Holmer Gre
HEROES OF WWI

This book has been published as part of an ongoing WWI Centenary project to keep the memory alive of the Holmer Green men who fought and died in the First World War and are remembered on the village War Memorial. Stuart King and Chris Peers are two of the members of a project team which has been working since 2013 to identify the men behind the carved names on the Memorial stone – their lives, families, where they lived and where and how they died in the service of their country.

Holmer Green was a small village of around 150 buildings at the time of the 1911 census – homes, workshops, churches, pubs and school included. The loss of the fourteen men whose names are on the Memorial affected nearly everyone in this small community – and with so many more of their men away with the forces, each loss must have had a greater effect and increase in concern for those still fighting.

A tremendous amount of research has been done by the project team and by the staff and students of Holmer Green Senior School. Family histories have been researched to find the homes and occupations of the villagers at the start of the war and to identify the many family links that tied them together into one community. Along the way it was decided that the book should also add to the village's own history and include bits and pieces that help show how people lived and worked at that momentous time in history.

The stories related in these pages have been collected from the memories of residents, gathered and passed on over many decades. Stuart and Chris have done their best to verify these memories and to minimise the distortions that passing time and word of mouth can create. However, the team recognises the certainty that as soon as this book is published there will be a rush of people coming forward to add to the tale or to point out every perceived error. It is hoped that all this content will become available online in an electronic format that can be added to and enhanced with all new information – and corrected where necessary – so that this story of a small Buckinghamshire hilltop village and its Heroes of WWI will live on.

Stuart King & Christopher Peers

Supported by
The National Lottery®
through the Heritage Lottery Fund

heritage
lottery fund

First published in 2017 by Hawkes Design & Publishing Ltd.

Copyright © 2017 Hawkes Design & Publishing Ltd

Stuart King and Christopher Peers have asserted their moral right to be identified as the authors of this work.

ISBN: 978-0-9554707-8-3

CHAPTER I

From 'Heath' to 'Heroes'

In 2006 Holmer Green local historians Roland McLain-Smith and Paul Riches published a book covering the early history of the village entitled 'Once Upon a Heath' with a starting point beginning with Domesday and culminating in the enclosure award of 1854 – an Act of Parliament that redefined the layout of our village and reapportioned much ownership of land. This was a 'new beginning' in many ways for Holmer Green with the wonderfully ancient, organically ragged by-ways, tracks, and lanes redrawn as we recognise them today.

This book picks up loosely from where 'Heath' ends and travels to the period of the early 1920s with a clear emphasis on the war years and 'Heroes' of 1914-18. McLain-Smith and Riches state; *"The Enclosure Act for Holmer Green came very late in 1854 and the layout of the village we see today was the direct result of this Act. Watchet Lane, Wycombe Road, Browns Road, Spurlands End Road, Beech Tree Road, Earl Howe Road, Parish Piece, Orchard Way (Factory Street), Sheepcote Dell Road and many other subsidiary roads were hedged"*.

Schoolchildren on the common.

Thomas Bond, farmer.

Hay making at Hollands Farm.

Holmer Pond.

Many of the villagers were, or felt, disenfranchised. Some took direct action to vent their frustration and pulled up the newly planted straight hawthorn hedges, at other times pre-enclosure common land, now under the plough, was 'seeded' with thistle seed. The perceived right to erect a home on the heath had disappeared forever along with the entitlement to freely graze livestock and freedom to roam. Their compensation? Allotments for the poor – small vegetable plots in designated areas in the newly created Beech Tree Road, Earl Howe Road and Sheepcote Dell Road.

A shepherd talking to Tilbury children in Watchet Lane, overlooking Haleacre Wood.

Holmer Green Common c1905.

Beech Tree Road allotments.

William Dean's tennis racket manufacture employees, New Pond Road.

3

The Common with Green View and Peddles Cottage in the background, sheep were used to keep the grass down.

Out of the old Wycombe Heath (3,000 acres in total), Holmer Green was allotted just 4 acres for recreation such as cricket, football and social gatherings. This was termed The Recreation Ground with the perimeter road known as Recreation Drive – today we call it The Common. Village ponds were protected, they were an important source for watering horses. Holmer Pond was the most significant, some others were New Pond and Peddles, then there was (it is still there) the venerable 'sheep-dip' in Watchet Lane, referred to as 'Woodcocks Swilly' in 1742 and yes, used for washing sheep. Names such as Sheepcote Dell Road and Mutton Bottom allude to the importance of sheep rearing centuries ago, replaced by more arable and dairy farming plus the growing of fruit, particularly cherries.

We are very lucky to have access to some wonderful ancient woodland via a network of equally ancient footpaths. The well managed local beech woods provided much employment to tree fellers, pit sawyers, charcoal burners, hurdle makers and chair bodgers. In the nineteenth century, chair bodging – the turning of chair legs and components on a simple pole lathe – was by far the largest village occupation. Pimp and faggot (for fire lighting) making was an ancillary craft using the small waste wood. It was usual to set up one's simple equipment in situ in the woodland but unusually Holmer Green chair bodgers preferred working at home, entailing the carting of large trunks of beech to workplaces. Many of these chair leg turners supplied the local chair factory Dancer and Hearn in Factory Street (now Orchard Way) from the late 19th century through to the 1920s, probably the largest local employer.

Dancer and Hearne's chairmaking employees, Factory Street.

Other cottage crafts included straw-plait and lace making, later to be replaced by tambour beading, referred to as 'bead-work'. Minnie King was an agent who would organise the work and deliver completed items to the London 'rag trade' every Friday. Local entrepreneurs included Fred Tucker whose bakery business (started 1861) was still family run, well after a century of trading. Fred with his wife Rhoda also ran the village post office and at the turn of the 20th century he was investing his profits in building homes to rent, some in Earl Howe Road. Sam Beal had a sweet shop and later a bicycle repair shop facing the common, he also did a little bit of photography. Mrs Miles opened her front room at Cherry Croft in the Earl Howe Road (opposite Holmer Pond) as a sweet shop saying she would be selling sweets cheaper than Sam Beal.

Holmer Green, in common with the wider area of our Chilterns, was a hot-bed for non-conformists and meetings were established in the village at least a century before the building of our Anglian 'Christ Church' in 1894. It appears that in the dying years of the 18th century in the long reign of George III, a weary traveller named Darvill from Chesham, walking up Penfold Lane, sought and received refreshment at a cottage close to where it meets the ancient trackway of Featherbed Lane.

Saunders' Chair Leg Factory, Bottom Alley, 1973

Making Bucks bobbin lace.

Mrs Lou Dean, tambour beading.

Our traveller was warmly welcomed and struck up a close friendship with the cottagers and was soon a frequent visitor, leading to regular Sunday cottage gatherings of worship, destined to develop into the Baptist Church. A simple Church and Sunday school was built c1830 and was replaced by an attractive 'neat and commodious' brick and flint structure built in 1869. This was extended in 1899 and again in1928.

John Wesley was the founder of Methodism, he died in 1791 and had long sowed the seeds of his beliefs locally. He preached at least twice to large crowds outside the little market house in High Wycombe after a long trek from Oxfordshire over the 'mountain' at Stokenchurch. Wesley's influence was profound and in common with virtually all Buckinghamshire villages, Holmer Green worshipers built a Methodist chapel in the Earl Howe Road in 1841 after meeting in a nearby cottage for at least twenty years before. Like the Baptists, the Methodist chapel has gone through several enlargements over the years and both churches are still thriving today. Before Christ Church was built in 1894, the same year in which little Missenden Parish council was established, worshipers would have to walk to Little Missenden church and back twice every Sunday.

Baptist Chapel, the Common.

Early Methodist Chapel, Earl Howe Road.

A group of young Sunday school attendees, Christ Church c1901.

RUPERT KING'S POEM

*Written on the opening of a new extension
to the Holmer Green Methodist Chapel.*

*Harken, there is much to tell
At Holmer Green they're doing well
Saving souls from going to hell,
And glory let it be so.*

~

*Our chapel holds the rustic throng,
To lift up voice in hopeful song,
Some will bring their fiddles along,
And glory let it be so*

~

*Brother James will rant and war,
While opening wide the door,
Shouting sinners, there's room for more!
And glory let it be so.*

~

*Brother Wingrove all complete,
In his cuffs and collar neat,
Showing sinners to their seat,
And glory let it be so.*

~

*Up and down treads brother Ayres,
Helping old folk up the stairs,
Keeping silence while in prayers,
And glory let it be so.*

~

*Brother Ware will have his say,
Brother Beal will watch and pray,
And scare the devil right away,
And glory let it be so*

~

*At Holmer Green they're doing well
Hear the alleluias swell,
Souls are being saved from hell,
And glory let it be so!*

First school building, built c1846 and pictured c1900.

Although both chapels held Sunday schools the first general school was established in the Beech Tree Road opposite the common. It was built with funds from an anonymous lady donor as a Church of England school with the proviso that it was open to any Christian denomination or none. Even so, some chapel going families preferred that their children attended a chapel school at Little Kingshill. The Holmer Green brick and flint building was replaced by another on the same site, with the foundation stone laid in March 1908 by the Bishop of Oxford and it served as a school until the 1920s. It serves us today as the Village Centre, our Village Hall.

The 'new' school' c1910.

The foundation stone of the new school 1908.

Mayday celebrations on the common, pre WWI.

There was no shortage of pubs including The Bat and Ball, The Beech Tree, The Earl Howe, The Black Horse, the Old Stag and Hounds, the New Stag and Hounds and for a short time The Fox – like all the others except for the Old Stag and Hounds it was a beer house. The 'Old Stag' had a spirit licence as it was here that the followers of Rothschild's of Waddesdon stag hounds drank after the chase. The stag was quite tame, brought along in a wheeled cage and released to leap away across country, often towards Penn Street where the hounds and riders caught up with it. The unharmed breathless animal was then re-caged to run another day leaving the toffs to indulge in their favourite spirit.

The Old Stag and Hounds pub with Minnie King, neé Hazel in doorway.

The New Stag and Hounds Pub with locals including Fred Tucker, baker, on far left.

Fox Cottage, a onetime beer-house in Fox Road.

So why another pub called the Stag and Hounds? Simply to try and entice some of the monied hunting crowd from the Old Stag.

Richard Tilbury built the Bat and Ball pub in the late 1820s. It was ideally located close to where several roads and tracks converged and almost certainly opposite an area of the heath used for sports and recreation long before it was officially designated as such in 1854. In the early 20th century the then landlord, Alfred Tilbury, applied for a spirit license, citing the unfair advantage that the 'Old Stag' had, but was unsuccessful on this occasion.

The Beech Tree pub was built just after enclosure and took advantage of a newly established crossroads, the name reflecting the local beech woods close by and the village chair leg turners for whom the beech woods supplied their raw material. The Earl Howe pub, one might surmise was named possibly to ingratiate the premises with the local lord of the manor, Earl Howe's many estate workers, or maybe in recognition of a munificent overlord?

The Black Horse, 1910.

The Old Beech Tree, 1963

Maurice Wingrove (right), landlord of The Earl Howe

The Earl Howe Pub.

The Tuckers domain. Fred Senior with wife Rhoda and children talking to traveling reps from Kinghams of Watford – suppliers to the Post Office and general stores run by Rhoda, Fred ran the bakers next door.

Much of the fantastic advances in engineering, exploration, architecture and inventions of the nineteenth century passed our tiny village by. There was the short-lived upheaval of the 1854 enclosure but the quiet village way of life adapted and changed little. There was some expansion towards the end of the 19th century and into the early 20th when local business people such as shopkeeper and baker Fred Tucker and the Salter greengrocer family were building new homes.

The Post Office was in Bottom Alley – Post Office Road did not exist.

Rhoda outside the Post Office and Fred outside the Bakers.

Fred Tucker had money to spare as he also built speculative houses for rent in the Earl Howe Road – the Laurels, Ivy Cottages and Holly Cottages – an early example of ribbon development. These were brick built homes and a departure from the homelier cottages comprising of warm orange bricks and flint.

Hill View, The Tucker's house in the Beech Tree Road.

Holly Cottages, Earl Howe Road.

Joseph Keen's forge and wheelwrights shop in Earl Howe Road with John Salter's cart in for repair. The building still exists.

Chair Leg turner Alan Dean in his garden workshop in Spurlands End Road. His father Charles was a chair bodger living next door to the Tilbury family in 'Langstons' cottage on Howe Hill, Watchet Lane.

Old Shepherds Hut, Wycombe Heath, Holmer Green.

Alley Mansions now Crossways – Pond Approach.

Wycombe Heath windmill built by Job Pearce 1829 with miller's daughter Polly Leach sat on the gate.

Frederick, Elizabeth and Polly Leach, the miller's family by their cottage on Wycombe Heath.

Harry Wingrove's orchard, Watchet Lane, now Harries Way.

Holmer Green fruit pickers, great skill was required in manoeuvring these extremely tall ladders.

Blue Bonnet Cottage, formerly a Drovers Pub, Spurlands End.

Mill End cottages, always referred to as The Four Houses – Watchet Lane.

CHAPTER 2

George Cross

This story begins in the mid-19th century when a tinker, formerly from Chedworth, Gloucestershire, was climbing Hamilton Hill after drinking too much at High Wycombe fair and was sleeping it off by the side of the road. Abraham 'Tinker' Evans was offered help from a Hazelmere girl called Mary Ann, they married and lived in a small single storied cottage at 'Cuckoo Town'. 'Cuckoo Town' was an ironic epithet for a small cluster of mostly squatter's cottages close to the top of Watchet Lane known as 'Howe Hill'. In 1881 there were nine Evans family members including 2 grandchildren living under one roof.

Abraham was a true tinker, he made and repaired metal pots and pans which Mary Ann would then sell at local markets in Amersham, Chesham and High Wycombe and bring back others for repair, walking all the way. After living in the cottage for many years Tinker Evans refused to pay any more rent and the family were evicted. His farming neighbour at next door Wycombe Heath Farm, Thomas Winter, took pity and offered a small corner plot if some form of accommodation could be found. This problem was solved by one of Tinker's sons, Joseph, who travelled to London and brought back an obsolete horse drawn bus. This was to serve the Evans' adequately for many years. Tinker lived out his days in that old bus and his wife was still there in the early 1920s, by this time she was well known as Granny Evans. Their daughter Emma married a local lad Owen Cross and set up home in

'Tinker' Evans with his wife Mary Ann sitting outside the old London Horse Drawn bus that became their home for many years in a field belonging to Thomas Winter of Wycombe Heath Farm.

Dormer Lane close by. Each day Emma would walk across Winters field taking pails of water to her until eventually Granny Evans went to live in the Dormer Lane cottage with her daughter.

One of a number of squatters cottages at 'Cuckoo Town', Watchet Lane, this may have been the original Holmer Green home of the Evans'. Seen here with a Mrs Lawrence in the doorway.

14

Although he is not remembered on the Holmer Green War Memorial, another casualty was Frederick John Beasley. Frederick was born in Holmer Green in 1870 to Emma Beasley who was living next door to Tinker Evans in 'Cuckoo Town' with her parents, siblings and Alice – Emma's illegitimate daughter. Frederick was also illegitimate.

In adulthood, Frederick became a navvy, working as a labourer on large construction projects and in 1901 he was in Woking, Surrey, where he was helping to build a large cemetery which would provide a resting place for many of London's dead, delivered by railway.

By 1911, Frederick was married and he and his wife, Ellen, were living in Hughenden with two children which he supported by general labouring.

When war came, Frederick enlisted into the Oxfordshire & Buckinghamshire Light Infantry but was later transferred to the 2nd Battalion of the Hampshire Regiment. With the Hampshires he was to travel to Gallipoli in Turkey where he was killed in action on 6th August 1915 during the fighting to break out from the landing area.

Frederick has no known grave but is remembered on the Helles Memorial in Turkey. He is also remembered on a memorial stone on the wall of the Holmer Green Baptist Church – Frederick probably attended the Baptist Church Sunday School as a boy whilst growing up in the village.

Also remembered on the Baptist Church stone is George Frederick Mason who before the war lived at Mop End Farm where he worked the farm with his father, Charles Alfred Mason.

Like Frederick Beasley, George Mason enlisted early on in the war and joined the Royal Buckinghamshire Hussars with whom he too went to Gallipoli where he was killed in action on 21st August 1915. He was only 18 so must have lied about his age as soldiers under 19 were not permitted to serve overseas.

George also has no known grave and is remembered on the Helles Memorial in Turkey and also on the Penn Street War Memorial.

George Cross was born in October 1891 and was named Owen after his father but was always known by his middle name of George. He was the second child of eleven children born to Owen Cross and Emma Evans who he had married in 1889. Owen had grown up in Little Kingshill, brought up with his elder brother Arthur by their mother Sarah after the early death of their father. By the age of 15, Owen was working as a ploughboy at Sedges Farm on Nags Head Lane. He was still working there in 1891 but was now living in a cottage with Emma and their new born daughter, named Emma. Here they also had Owen George and Elsie.

They then moved briefly to Terriers where another daughter, Olive May, was born but by the turn of the century, Owen and Emma had moved to the Dormer Lane cottage at the Wycombe Heath end of Holmer Green. Owen was working as a Woodman and Florence Rose had joined the family. The 1911 census shows that they were still in Wycombe Heath (Dormer Lane) and Mary Ethel, Abraham William, Ernest Arthur, Mabel Sarah and Amy Grace had arrived to complete the family.

The brick and flint cottage in Dormer Lane where several generations of the Evans offspring, namely the Cross families, lived.

Emma Cross, nee Evans
at Dormer Lane.

The Dormer Lane cottage.

The young George was no longer at the family home and was presumably making his living outside the local area – possibly in Berkshire as George enlisted in Reading, Berkshire at the start of the Great War and after training was posted to the Berkshire Regiment and is likely to have been serving overseas by the summer of 1915. At some point he was wounded and upon discharge from the Medical Reception Station discovered that his regiment had been moved elsewhere in the line. However, the 2nd Battalion of the King's Own Yorkshire Light Infantry were billeted nearby and he was assigned to them as a stretcher bearer.

In 1916, this Battalion was in the 97th Brigade, part of the 32nd Division on the Somme sector of the Western front. It had been heavily involved in the assault on the first day of the Somme offensive on 1st July and had lost 349 officers and other ranks killed, wounded and missing in that day's fighting.

Once relieved on 2nd July the survivors pulled back to their bivouac at Contay Wood to rest and clean up. A & B Companies were combined into one company, as were C & D Companies and it was in this half strength state that they went back into the front line on 9th July. Here they stayed until 16th July, being shelled constantly and participating in night-time raids on the enemy trenches.

This pattern of rest and refit followed by periods in the front line trenches continued into August when they were pulled back to be part of the Divisional Reserve to focus on refit and training for three weeks. Then they went back into the line at Bethune. On 14th October they were relieved and received a draft of 100 men – the majority of whom were new conscripts with no battle experience. Over the next eight days the battalion marched in stages to a new bivouac at Bouzincourt, commencing training and practice attacks on 25th October. Then on 31st October they marched to La Vicogne for more drill and training until 13th November when they moved to Contay in preparation for the start of the battle of the Ancre.

Initially expecting to take part in a dawn attack on the 15th, instead the battalion moved a relatively short distance to Englebelmer – adjacent to Beaumont-Hamel where so many men had died on 1st July. At 10.00pm on the 16th they went up to the front line trenches in readiness for an attack the following night. The 97th Brigade lined up with George's KOYLI battalion on the left, then 11th Borders, 16th Highland Light Infantry and then 17th Highland Light Infantry on the right. To the 97th's left, the 14th Brigade would carry out a defensive flank movement and the rest of 32nd Division would be attacking on their right. 96th Brigade was behind them in support. Late on the 17th the line moved out from the trench to an advanced line which had been marked out by Royal Engineers – ahead lay the Munich Trench, which would be the battalion's first objective at dawn on the 18th.

Weather conditions were bad and it started snowing just before the attack – at 6.10am an intense British barrage commenced and the enemy fired off several Very lights which lit up the now white ground that the British had to cross. The line advanced and on the left succeeded in reaching the Munich trench but the right was held up by intense machine gun and rifle fire and went to ground in a line of shell holes in front of the German wire. The left side continued their attack and after some heavy fighting, occupied a section of the Frankfurt trench – their final objective for the day. A few reinforcements and a supply of bombs were sent up to the left but the right was still held up. On the KOYLI's right, the 11th Borders had retired having also failed to progress and so the order was given to withdraw to the start trench. It was now 6.30pm and the battalion was reduced to the Colonel, Adjutant, Intelligence Officer, one 2nd Lieutenant and 170 other ranks. At 10.00pm the battalion was relieved by the 11th Lancashires and returned to billet in Mailley-Maillet. News came through that a Lieutenant and some men from the left flank companies were cut off but still holding on in a section of the Frankfurt trench, however, all attempts to reach and relieve them had proved impossible.

At some point during this action on the 18th November, Private Owen George Cross, together with another stretcher bearer and the man they were trying to carry to safety, were hit by an artillery shell and killed. He has no known grave but is remembered on the Thiepval Memorial. He was 25 years old.

George's effects were valued at £30.15s.4d which was paid to his Mother, Emma, on 2nd June 1917 – Emma also received a War Gratuity of £13.00.

The Holmer Green Royal British Legion Standard at the Thiepval Memorial 2016.

The Thiepval Memorial.

Pete Rolt, nephew of Owen George Cross, laying a Holmer Green Heroes wreath in memory, 2016.

CHAPTER 3

Frederick Thomas Haystaff

The youngest child of John and Frances Louisa Haystaff, Frederick was born in July 1896 in Marlow, Buckinghamshire. His father John came from Aylesbury where generations of the Haystaff family had lived for at least 200 years. In 1881 John and his younger brother Frederick as young men of 17 and 15 were living with their grandparents – John, a retired Milkman and his wife Charlotte - probably helping to care for the elderly couple and with their wages as a Groom and Errand Boy no doubt contributing to the household.

In 1887 John married Frances Louisa North and the 1891 census records John and Louisa living in High Wycombe – John is now a Police Constable with the County Constabulary and they already have 3 little children - John, Edith and Gertrude. John's postings continue to move the family around and their daughter Florence is born in Gerrards Cross, then comes the posting to Marlow where Frederick Thomas Haystaff is born and presumably named after John's younger brother.

In the early 1900s John was posted to be Holmer Green's village policeman and moved into the Westbourne Cottages in Factory Street (now Orchard Way) with his family - this short terrace still exists. The 1911 census shows the 14 year old Frederick at home there with his parents and 16 year old sister Florence.

We lose track of Frederick for a while then, we don't know what trade he took up – perhaps he became a policeman like his father, or did he work in the local chair trade like many of his neighbours? The next we know of him is when he joined the army, probably in 1915.

Frederick Haystaff enlisted in Brackley, Northamptonshire and became a member of the Northamptonshire Regiment. We don't know exactly when Frederick was posted abroad but certainly in the summer of 1916 he was serving with B Company of the 1st Battalion of the Northampton-shire Regiment as it played it's part in the Somme battles.

In late July and early August 1916 the battalion was billeted firstly near Albert and then at Henencourt Wood. Here their days were spent with parades, tug of war competitions, relay races – and a number of training exercises particularly on attack and deployment against hostile trench lines as well as practice night assaults.

Then, on 13th August the battalion – having completed all tasks and made all necessary arrangements – left Henencourt and marched by platoons to a space of open ground between Albert and Bicourt Wood where they stayed for the night. The morning of the 14th was spent with games and races and then at 2.30pm they moved off in platoons to relieve the 16th Royal Scots who were in support trenches on the left of High Wood.

The relief was hampered by enemy shellfire throughout the evening and night and the battalion counted itself fortunate to only suffer 4 casualties during the move and a further 5 whilst digging in and expanding the trenches overnight.

Orchard Way, formerly Factory Street.

15th August was spent resting until 5.00pm when they moved forward to relieve the 2nd Royal Sussex in the front line. Two patrols were sent out to scout the enemy positions and based on their reports it was decided to launch a surprise attack without any preparatory fire – however this was beaten back with a number of casualties.

At 9.25am on the 16th, one of the Lieutenants who had been part of the night attack returned after spending some time between the lines, sheltering in shell holes. The information he had gathered from observing the enemy positions made him absolutely confident of success should the regiment attack again - and he offered his services to lead that attack. Attack plans were made, orders issued and at 10.50pm C & D Companies together with elements of the 2nd Royal Sussex made a successful attack to capture a portion of the enemy trenches. The Royal Sussex were ultimately driven out of their section by German counter-attacks but C Company resisted all attacks and held although Lieutenant Nye – whose information had led to the attack being made – was killed in the defence, one of 42 casualties from this day's actions.

17th August was spent consolidating the ground taken and A Company succeeded in capturing the rest of the trench line in their sector despite taking a total of 112 casualties, killed, wounded or missing.

In the afternoon of the 18th and with the support of two mortars, the battalion succeeded in bombing down and re-taking the section to their right which had been taken and lost by the Royal Sussex. Simultaneously with this attack, A Company launched a flanking attack to their left in support of a frontal attack by the Royal North Lancashires which succeeded in capturing that section of the line. During the following day outposts were established on the ridgeline in front of these new positions but then during the night a party of about 50 Germans got into the position from High Wood and in the confused fighting in the dark the battalion lost a further 14 men.

PC Haystaff's wife and daughter, mother and sister of Frederick outside their terrace cottage 'Westbourne' in Orchard Way (formerly Factory Street).

NAME AND SURNAME	RELATIONSHIP to Head of Family.	AGE (last Birthday) and SEX.		PARTICULARS as to MARRIAGE.				
		Ages of Males.	Ages of Females.		Completed years the present Marriage has lasted.	Total Children Born Alive.	Children still Living.	Children who have Died.
1 John Haystaff	Head	48		Married	24	6	5	1
2 Frances Louisa Haystaff	Wife		53	Married				
3 Florence May Haystaff	Daughter		16	Single				
4 Frederick Hⁿ Haystaff	Son	14						
5								
6								

1911 census, Frederick Haystaff living in Holmer Green.

The Thiepval Memorial.

At 7.00am on the 20th August, the Germans mounted a determined attack against the outpost positions, pushing them back off the ridgeline. Frederick's B Company now became directly involved in the battle as they led the counter-attack, supported by A Company. The fighting lasted all morning but then the Companies regrouped and after a rather ineffectual artillery barrage, at 2.30pm B and A Companies together with two companies of the Royal Sussex went out again.

After a very severe fight they succeeded in establishing an outpost about 800 metres in front of the newly taken trenches from which an excellent view of the enemy's positions and troop movements was obtained and artillery fire could be directed. This position was consolidated and then handed over to the 2nd Welsh who relieved the 1st Northamptonshire during the night. They made their way back behind the front line, returning to their bivouac at Bicourt Wood at about 4.00am on the 21st.

The thanks and congratulations of the High Command were passed to the Regiment for a particularly brilliant and glorious period of this attack. All the objectives were taken and held and despite heavy losses the spirit and tenacity of the Regiment were maintained.

Private Frederick Thomas Haystaff of B Company was killed in action on the 20th of August, almost certainly in either the initial counter-attack or in the following push to capture the ridgeline. He was one of 138 casualties from those attacks and has no known grave but is remembered on the Thiepval Memorial. He was 20 years old.

His father, John, received £3.1s.4d on 5th September 1917 as the value of Frederick's effects and a War Gratuity of £3.10s.0d on 22nd September 1919.

A strong contingent from the Northampton Branch of the East Anglian Regimental Association came to remember their comrade in September 2016.

CHAPTER 4

Ralph James

Ralph James was born in January 1886 in Holmer Green, the fourth of eleven children by Jethro James and his wife, Emma Pearce. Jethro was a Wood turner and he and Emma lived in a cottage in No. 2 Factory Street (now Orchard Way). Jethro's father, George, was also in the chair manufacture trade, a chair leg turner, and had also been born in Holmer Green – in fact this branch of the James family had been in the village since at least the mid-1700s. Prior to the creation of the cottages and workshops in Factory Street, George had lived in Two Hedges (now New Pond Road), in a cottage opposite the Black Horse, about where the Rossetti Hall stands now.

Above: No.2 Factory Street (now Orchard Way) home of chair bodger Jethro James and his wife Emma, parents to Ralph.

Originally a pair of semi detached dwellings No.2 was here on the left-hand side, there would have been a wooden workshop in the back garden to house the pole lathe and other equipment plus timber storage.

New Pond Road, Granny James by the brick and flint cottage (left), the arrow below shows its position in the lane. The wooden clad building next door was Bill Dean's tennis racket factory.

When Ralph finished school he found work as a cowman at a farm in nearby Bellingdon and lived there as a boarder. His elder brothers were still at home in Holmer Green – Frank was a chair leg turner like Jethro but Harry had got into the new industry of tennis bat/racket manufacture working as a 'bat stringer'. The James name was becoming well known for tennis racket making but this was Bertie James who had a factory on Recreation Drive (now The Common) and we have not found any family connection between Ralph James' branch and Bertie – who himself was a cousin to another Holmer Green Hero, Wilfred James.

A connection is made though by another of Ralph's brothers, Gilbert, who married Ruth Salter in July 1909. Ruth lost two of her brothers in the war – Harold and Ernest – two more of our Heroes.

Ralph was probably called up in early 1917, attested in Chesham to the 3rd Reserve Battalion of the local Regiment – the Oxford and Buckinghamshire Light Infantry. After basic training he went initially to join the OBLI 6th Battalion before being posted on to the regiment's 5th Battalion in the France and Flanders theatre, joining them on 6th July 1917.

Ralph James' grave, Westhof Farm Cemetery.

The Battalion was in billets at Vert Glant, near Amiens, where the focus was on training and the impending football final between OBLI and the King's Shropshire Light Infantry. This match was first played on 8th July and finished 1 – 1, necessitating a replay on 10th July. This resulted in another draw, 0 – 0, this time – and then the war intervened with honours even on the pitch as the Battalion entrained the next morning for new billets at Bailleul. Here the emphasis was on specialist training including contact patrols and co-operative work with the Royal Flying Corps – using flares to direct their ground strikes.

This training continued until mid-August when they started to get organised for an attack, moving forward to the front line in the Glencorse Wood sector on 17th August. However, the trench line they occupied was in poor condition from enemy shelling and they were themselves extensively shelled once in position. This bombardment continued for the next few days and nights and then overnight on the 23rd/24th, the Germans launched bombing attacks on the sections to the OBLI's flanks. The Germans were using a sap trench to reach the British positions and set up a strongpoint in it – this was attacked by the Duke of Cornwall's Light Infantry assisted by two Companies of the OBLI, one of which was Ralph's 'C' Company who made bombing attacks on the enemy held trench. After some hard fighting within the British trenches, the enemy were eventually driven out and back to their own lines, although British snipers took a heavy toll of the retreating men. Following this the Battalion was relieved from the front line, having lost 8 Officers and 286 Other Ranks Killed, Wounded or Missing.

*Cowman Ralph James attired in his Oxford
and Buckinghamshire Light Infantry uniform.*

The Flanders Fields where Ralph James lost his life, he lies close by in the tiny Westhof Farm Cemetery, Belgium.

After a few days rest and reorganisation they marched to Neuve Englise on 1st September and went back into the trenches on the 2nd. The Battalion was kept busy, improving their trenches and digging new communication trenches with only occasional shelling to interrupt them. They were relieved on 10th September and moved periodically to different camps over the next couple of weeks whilst training and refitting during a period of hot, sunny weather.

The 27th of September 1917 was scheduled to be another quiet day of training exercises before the Battalion would march on the following day to relieve the 6th King's Own Yorkshire Light Infantry in the front line. Lewis Gunner sections spent most of the day on the firing range but otherwise the billet lines were undisturbed – until about 9.45pm when a German aircraft was heard overhead and the billet area was bombed.

One bomb dropped straight on a 'C' Company hut and killed six men and wounded thirteen more. When the Battalion moved out at 7.00am the following morning, Ralph James did not go with them. He is buried in the small cemetery behind Westhof Farm – a piece of land on a hill with a commanding view over the fields and copses all around. Alongside him lie the other five men killed in the hut that night – Lance Corporal Champ and Privates Eastment, Oakley, Payne and Smedley.

Westhof Farm was the scene of much heavy fighting during 1917 and 1918, it had served as the New Zealand Division's Headquarters for a while and for five months it had been occupied by the Germans as part of their front line. The cemetery holds 136 men from many regiments and countries who are buried there, both friend and foe.

Ralph's effects were valued at £3.16s.1d which was paid to his Mother, Emily, on 23 January 1918. After the war the Government also paid her a War Gratuity of £3.0s.0d on 22 November 1919.

CHAPTER 5

Wilfred James

This branch of the James family has been in Holmer Green since at least the mid-18th century, John James was born in the village in March 1767, married a Holmer Green girl, Elizabeth Messer, and they had ten children. Their seventh child was Edmond, born in July 1802, he married Sarah Sibley in 1820 and they too had ten children.

A Bertie James Tennis Racket with makers transfer intact – note the postal address is Amersham.

Their fifth child – and first born son after four daughters – was born in 1828 and called Edmond after his father. This Edmond married Emma Brown in 1854 and amazingly they also had ten children. The eighth of these was Bertie who came along in 1873 and he married Bertha Lacey in 1894. Bertie would become well known as a manufacturer of tennis rackets, owning one of two factories in the village dedicated to these items.

Bertie and Bertha had three children, the middle one being Wilfred who was born in October 1898. Edmond and Emma lived in Two Hedges (now New Pond Road) – near to the Black Horse and the Old Stag and Hounds, Bertie and Bertha though had set up home and business at No.1 Recreation Drive which was the road that circled the Recreation Ground – now both road and ground are known as The Common. Bertie's house was just to the west of where the Junior School is now sited.

Bertie James' cottage in Recreation Drive (now The Common) and overlooking the common, formerly 'the Recreation Ground' and named such from the time of Parliamentary enclosure. Wilfred's father Bertie learnt his tennis racket making trade working for Bill Dean before setting up on his own – he is seen here outside his home still wearing his working apron.

Wilfred was called up around May 1917 and enlisted at Aylesbury where he was posted to the Royal Warwickshire Regiment. Later on he would join the 8th Battalion Royal Berkshire Regiment with whom he was serving when he was killed. The Royal Warwickshire Regiment had several home based battalions to which new recruits were posted for training and it may be that Wilfred was posted from one of these to the Royal Berkshire Regiment when he went overseas for active service. If so he probably arrived in time for the Second Battle of Passchendale in October and November 1917.

Bertie James in working apron, probably with one of his sons, either Cecil or Bertie — no other images are known of Bertie's children.

In early April 1918 the battalion was in the front line at Gentelles when it was subjected to a major German barrage and attack. The wounding or death of their commanding officers in succession meant that by 6.00pm on 4th April, command of the battalion had devolved down to a Lieutenant before they were given orders to withdraw. The following weeks were spent in camp, receiving and bedding in new officers and large drafts of replacements for those lost. In all, 16 officers and 589 men joined the battalion this month.

By the end of May they were back in the front line, moving to different sections of the Somme sector during June and July. On 1st August 1918 the battalion was in the reserve trenches in front of La Houssoye near Beauvais. On the evening of 6th August the battalion moved forward to take up position in a sunken road in front of Heilly to the east of Amiens where they stayed through the daylight hours of the 7th until as dusk fell they moved to assembly positions in the Roma Line, the jump off point for their part in the first day of the Battle of Amiens.

At 4.20am on 8th August the British artillery opened a barrage on the enemy positions and the battalion moved forward in platoons behind it. A thick mist hung over the battlefield and progress was slow as the direction of advance had to be continually checked by the compasses held by each platoon. The German artillery opened fire but were shooting blind because of the conditions and so were firing at previously sighted in locations and the battalion made progress with relatively light casualties from the shellfire.

Contact was made on the right with parties of German troops in an old front line trench in front of the main trench, these troops were supported by two heavy machine guns and the Royal Berkshire platoons that found them became disoriented and came to a different section of trench where they again came under fire from more machine guns. On the left of the advance, the Berkshires and other units from their Brigade succeeded in reaching their objectives – a ravine beyond the enemy trench. They had expected other troops and some tanks to be ahead of them but they were the first units to make it there which

they did at about 7.40am. From here they continued their advance – still in poor visibility until the mist cleared away. They were then immediately engaged by heavy machine gun fire at close range which was simultaneously joined by the fire of two field guns who were close enough to be firing over open sights at the British. Three attempts were made to rush these gun positions but these were ineffective in the face of the enemy fire and ultimately they withdrew to form a line level with the ravine they had earlier occupied. From here, the Regiment's commanding officer led a flank attack on the enemy positions which was also beaten off, the CO being wounded in the attack.

That evening Brigade HQ issued orders for the battalion to withdraw from the line for re-organisation, each of the four companies forming just two platoons each from the men left fit to fight.

Private Wilfred James died on the 8th of August – he was wounded in the fighting but his wounds proved fatal and he died later the same day and is recorded as being killed in action. He is buried in the Beacon Cemetery in Sailly-Laurette on the Somme. It is likely that he was initially buried in an impromptu graveyard alongside a casualty treatment centre and then moved to the Beacon Cemetery in 1919 when graves from several of the smaller burial grounds in the area were brought there.

His effects were valued at £9.16s.4d which was paid to his mother, Bertha, on 4th March 1919 and a War Gratuity of £5.00 was also paid to Bertha on 2nd January 1920.

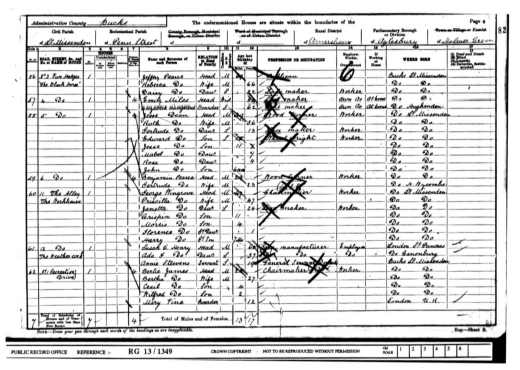

The 1901 Census showing the James family living at No. 1 Recreation Drive.

CHAPTER 6

Merrick Hugh McConnel

Merrick McConnel was born on 6th November 1884, the eldest of five children by William Houldsworth McConnel and Florence Bannister. Merrick was born in BlaenauFfestiniog in Merionethshire, Wales where his father was a Director of a mining company and Secretary of a railway company although the family shortly thereafter moved residence to Leicester Grange in Wolvey, Warwickshire.

Merrick's education started at the St Thomas Boarding School in Southampton, then to Horris Hill School in Newbury and thence to Winchester College. Here he was a House Prefect and a noted player of cricket and Association football and was rated as one of the best racquets players. He won the college Steeplechase – a cross-country running event. He was a good violinist and as a boy was said to possess a beautiful voice. In 1902 he passed into the Royal Military Academy in Woolwich where he maintained his reputation as an athlete and in 1904 obtained his commission in the Royal Artillery.

He served in England for eight years including a period as Aide-De-Camp to Major-General H. E. Belfield, General Officer Commanding at Woolwich. Merrick married the Major-General's eldest daughter, Mary Clare

Merrick Hugh McConnel

Belfield, in the summer of 1912. Shortly thereafter Merrick was posted to India with his battery and was serving there when war broke out. Mary went with her new husband to India and their daughter Helen was born in Lucknow, India in 1913. In October 1914 he was ordered to France in command of an ammunition column and served there continuously until his death with the exception of two brief periods of ill-health. Mary and Helen returned to England, probably around the start of the war, and set up home in Polydores House, Holmer Green.

Polidoris Lane and Rossetti Place are now where Polydores House once stood.

Beech Tree road looking west.

The McConnel family's Holmer Green home replaced the earlier cottage that provided refuge to an Italian exile, one Gaetano Polidori, late secretary to Count Alffori. Gaetano was the grandfather of two of the most famous artists/poets of the 19th century, Christina and Gabriel Dante Rossetti, he of the Pre-Raphaelite Brotherhood of Ford Maddox Brown, Burne Jones, Millais and William Morris. The Rossetti Children would stay with their grandfather during the 1830s traveling from their Bloomsbury London home by stage coach and alighting at Little Missenden, then making their way to the village along Penfold Lane. Frustratingly no image has surfaced of the McConnel's home although it was named after Gaetano Polidori.

Merrick was twice Mentioned in Despatches during his time in France and Flanders. By September 1917 he had attained the rank of Major and was serving with B Battery of 295 Brigade which moved into a new position just east of Ypres during the night of 6th/7th September. By the morning of the 9th the batteries had completed registration firing – the marking of various targets and fixing of firing co-ordinates to facilitate rapid target location during an action. A night bombardment programme was carried out on the night of 10th/11th and then a practice bombardment conducted on the 11th where the batteries practised rolling barrages, advancing the fire in 200 metre steps.

That night 285 and 296 Brigade Artillery gave support to a Company from 126th Infantry Brigade who were seeking to capture a strongpoint and consolidate a section of the line. Merrick's B/295 battery was targeted on the Zonnebeke Redoubt and was ordered, on observation of three green Very lights (flares), to fire a salvo every 10 seconds for 7 minutes and then to cease fire to allow the infantry to go in. This was recorded in the war diary as 'minor night operation – successful barrage programme'.

A further practice barrage was scheduled for 13th September. B/295 was to target its 18 pounder guns on a specific section of the line and fire 3 rounds of shrapnel per minute per gun whilst six 4.5" howitzers were targeted on some old gun pits and were to fire 1.5 rounds per minute per gun of high explosive. The battery to commence firing at Zero Hour for three minutes and then to lift the range by 100 yards every 3 minutes thereafter, ceasing fire after 12 minutes.

An Observation Post was to be established at Frexenberg Crossroads – reported as an exposed position – and Major McConnel was ordered to oversee the observation and promptly submit his report on this barrage. The unit diary notes that this barrage operation commenced at 5.35pm on the 13th and that the officer observing – Major McConnel of B battery, 295 Brigade, was wounded whilst observing and died the next day – 14th September 1917. Apparently, during the action a German battery had engaged in counter fire on the exposed post and Merrick was hit by the shellfire.

Major Merrick Hugh McConnel is buried in Lijssenthoek Military Cemetery near Poperinge just west of Ieper (Ypres) in Belgium. The village of Lijssenthoek was situated on the main communication line between the Allied military bases in the rear and the Ypres battlefields. Close to the Front, but out of the extreme range of most German field artillery, it was a natural place to establish casualty clearing stations and Lijssenthoek became the largest evacuation hospital in the Ypres Salient. The cemetery is the second largest in the theatre with almost 11,000 graves and Merrick is probably buried quite close to where he succumbed to his wounds.

Merrick's Uncle – Captain Frederic Bradshaw McConnel – was presumably Merrick's executor as all of the monies were paid to him – £30 3s 5d for his effects paid on 10th January 1918 and £86 war gratuity paid on

Lijssenthoek Military Cemetery, Poperinge, Ypres Salient Battlefields, Belgium, the last resting place of Merrick Hugh McConnel.

Holmer Green Royal British Legion Standard Bearers commemorate the life and death of Merrick Hugh McConnel March 2016.

30th December 1919. Probate was completed on 13th November 1917 and Merrick's estate was totalled at £6,551 12s 6d.

Merrick's wife, Mary, moved from Holmer Green to Oxford where she died on 23rd March 1949 in Radcliffe Infirmary leaving an estate of £17,108 0s 7d.

CHAPTER 7

Charles Miles and John Miles

Charles and John were brothers, two of eight children born from the marriage between John Miles and Sophia Parsons – the Miles family have been living in and around Holmer Green since at least the early 1800s. Their father, John, was himself one of nine children, his father William having been born in the Beamond End side of the village in 1812. William had been a farm labourer throughout his working life and most of his sons also worked on the farms, but John became a chairmaker in his teens and carried this trade on into the twentieth century.

After their first child – Henry – was born, John and Sophia moved from Beamond End to a cottage in Brays Green Lane in Hyde Heath, near to where Sophia's parents lived and where Fred, Minnie and then Charles were born – Charles arriving on 3rd May 1888.

John and Sophia then moved again – this time to No. 2 Hunts Road (also known as Hunts Hill and Jock Hunts road, now Earl Howe Road) in Holmer Green where a little girl, Emma, was born in 1892 although sadly, she only lived for two hours. Then came John who was born in April 1894, followed by Cissie and Dora.

Charles and John's elder sister Minnie was married in 1909 to a Holmer Green man, Abel Palmer. Abel was to also lose two brothers in the war – John and Ephraim – so this couple suffered the grief of losing four brothers in three years. Many years later, Abel's sister, Sarah, also married into the Miles family. Sarah's first husband died in 1939 and then in 1941 she married Henry Miles, the eldest of John and Sophia's children.

Charles and John's mother, Sophia, died in February 1908 but a few months later, in November 1908, John

Cherry Croft, No.1 Earl Howe Road, opposite the pond and home in 1911 to John and Georgina Miles (in doorway) and their children Charles (22), John (17) and Dora (12). Georgina ran a sweet shop from her front room.

married Georgina Faulkner. Charles followed his father's trade and in 1911 as a twenty-two year old the census records him as a chairturner. The 1911 census shows John and Georgina now living at Cherry Croft, Holmer Green with Charles, seventeen year old John and twelve year old Dora. John was working as a grocer's assistant.

Traditional brick and flint cottages in Earl Howe Road.

Cherry Croft from across Holmer Pond showing a later hardware shop extension

Also living in Holmer Green at the time of the 1911 census was Charles and John's cousin Sidney George Miles who was in Westbourne Cottages, Factory Street (now Orchard Way) with his wife Sarah and their children. Sidney would also be killed in action on 15th June 1918 whilst fighting in Italy with the Oxford & Bucks Light Infantry and another cousin, Horace Miles, would be killed on 20th May 1918 whilst serving with the 179th Tunnelling Company in France.

Charles and John's elder brother Fred also fought, serving with the Devonshire Regiment in France until being invalided back to the UK. Their cousin, Christopher Miles, was also with the Ox & Bucks and returned safely at the end of the war.

The memorial information collected after the war separately records Charles and John as 'son of John Miles of 'Spinfield' Beach Road (sic Beech Tree Road), Holmer Green – so John must have moved again before 1920.

Spinfield, Beech Tree Road, now demolished but was opposite the Rosary and was the former home of John Miles, father of Henry and John. The right hand image was taken when it was Henry Miles' home, note the vegetable garden in the front.

Anne and William Miles

*The temporary cross and resting place of
Sidney George Miles*

Sidney George Miles with wife Sarah Ellen (seated with child) and family

*The Family of Horace Miles outside their home, Rose Cottage, Mop End
L-R: Rosie Lea, Alfred, Almeria, Sarah and Alice.*

Horace Miles.

Charles Miles attested at Aylesbury on 9th December 1915. He was measured at five feet eight inches tall and had a thirty six and a half inch chest. He was initially posted to 3/8th Battalion of the Royal Warwickshire Regiment – a training unit in England.

Charles joined the BEF in France on 11 June 1916 and was posted to 1/8 Royal Warwickshire Regiment, a Territorial battalion which had been there since March 1915.

The regiment took part in the first day of the Somme on 1st July 2016, going over the top with the first wave at 7.30am in the battle at Beaumont-Hamel. They quickly reached and took the first two enemy trench lines despite intense machine gun fire and heavy casualties. They then advanced again and captured the third line and from here mounted repeated bombing attacks on the fourth line – twice occupying it but unable to hold due to a lack of grenades coming up from the rear. Battalions from the second and third waves were so reduced in numbers when they reached the Royal Warwicks that they could only help consolidate the captured trenches and were not able to push on through. The battalion was then relieved and fell back to their bivouac area at Mailly-Mailly which they reached at 11.00am. In those few hours the unit had suffered casualties of 585 officers and men killed, wounded or missing.

They stayed there to rest and reorganise until 7th July and then moved to a new bivouac near Albert. Here they continued to rest and prepare until the 17th.

During the evening they moved up to the front line under enemy artillery fire which continued through the night as they relieved the defending unit and settled in, losing 47 men killed and wounded in the operation. The 18th and 19th were spent in the same trench and still under fire which caused 20 more casualties before they were relieved at 11.00pm on the 19th.

The regiment moved to a new bivouac at Boursincourt on the 20th and over the next couple of days received

Charles Miles.

drafts of replacements totalling 249 men. Then they moved in stages up to Ginchy and into the trench line at La Boiselle, arriving at 1.00am on 24th July. On the 25th they occupied support trenches near Pozieres and at 9.00am on 26th July 1916 the battalion was ordered to relieve the front line trenches.

It proved difficult to carry out this operation in daylight and a number of casualties were incurred before the relief was completed at about 5.00pm.

Miles Chair Works, Squirrel Pub Yard Penn Street Bob Miles far left, Fishy Wingrove far right.

Cyril Miles.

At 9.00pm that night, two parties of men with grenades were sent to carry out bombing attacks on the enemy trench. The right hand party initially bombed their way some 200 yards along the German trench before being pushed back 100 yards by counter attacks where they held and consolidated their position with a barrier. The left hand party progressed some 50 yards before coming up against a strongpoint guarding a junction. Many attempts were made to take this but without success and they were eventually bombed out and back to their start position.

At 3.00am on what was now the 27th July, another bombing party was sent to reinforce the barrier and then mounted more attacks down the right hand trench. The Germans strongly counter attacked twice, pushing the men back to the barrier but were unable to push the Warwicks back out of the captured trench.

That evening at 7.00pm the 7th Middlesex commenced the relief of the battalion who returned to their bivouac.

During the bombing attacks on the 26th and 27th the unit had lost 6 men killed and 41 wounded. Originally Charles Miles was described as 'wounded & missing', but this was later changed to 'died on 27th July 1916'.

Charles had served 232 days in the Army – 185 in the UK and 47 in France. He was 28 years old. As he has no known grave, Charles is commemorated on the Thiepval Memorial. Charles' effects came to a total of £3.11s.8d which was the sum paid to his father, John, on 1st September 1917. On 7th October 1919 John also received a War Gratuity of £3.0s.0d in respect of Charles' service.

Horace Miles, back right.

John Miles

John Miles was called up on 3rd August 1915 – his papers were delivered by a Mr H.E.Fellows who would perform the same service upon another of the village's men, Martin Stevens. Both John and Martin would be in the Coldstream Guards and both would be killed in action.

When John joined his records show that he was five feet eleven and one eighth inches in height with a chest measurement of thirty-five and a quarter inches – which expanded to thirty-seven and three-quarter inches, a tall and strong man of his day.

John was based in the UK until 6th June 1916 whilst undergoing training and then posted to France on 7th June 1916 – just four days before his brother Charles also embarked – to join the British Expeditionary Force as a member of the 1st Battalion, Coldstream Guards. The next major battle for the Coldstreams would be the Battle of Flers-Courcelette which would start at 6.20am on 15th September 1916.

In preparation for this, on 9th September 1916 the battalion moved up to Happy Valley – a camp behind the lines near Morlancourt, arriving about 6.15pm. The unit diary noted that the accommodation in tents was very scanty and the billeting area had been left in a very dirty state – clearly not to Guards standard. The 10th was a Sunday and taken up with church services – and on Monday 11th they cleaned up the camp.

Then the following day the battalion paraded at 6.30pm and marched to relieve the 1st Battalion of the Irish

Lieutenant Robert Deering of the 1st Battalion Coldstream Guards, reading the eulogy at John Miles' Centenary Memorial Service held on 11th September 2016.

Guards who were in billet at Carnoy, arriving about 8.30pm. The diary records that they arrived to find very insufficient accommodation for the battalion or its officers. A few bivouacs and half a dozen small dugouts were all that could be found. Here they rested on the 13th.

On 14th September the battalion paraded at 9.30pm in attacking order and marched to relieve the 2nd Battalion Irish Guards south east of Ginchy and to get into position for an attack the following morning – a long and difficult march meaning they were only in position in the assembly trenches at 2.45am. No. 3 and No. 4 Companies were in the first line trench. John was with No. 1 Company who along with No. 2 Company were lying out behind the trench in shell holes, taking cover from an intense German artillery barrage.

Tanks were being used by the British Army for the first time and had been distributed along the line. These were to precede the main assault, going forward at 5.30am behind an artillery barrage. Unfortunately for the battalion, the two tanks allocated to their position failed to arrive and the barrage only served to warn the Germans of the attack – the Germans started a counter barrage at 6.10am which caused a great many casualties.

The main British barrage now started at 6.20am along the whole line as the assault began and the troops went over the top to advance 30 yards behind this creeping barrage as it moved towards the German lines. To the 1st Coldstream's left were the 2nd and 3rd Coldstream battalions and these three units moved forward together – to maintain contact with the 2nd the 1st had to advance half-left but was now unfortunately caught by the British barrage and again suffered a good many casualties as a consequence.

According to the battle plan, the battalion's first objective was supposed to be 1,000 yards ahead, however the enemy were actually strongly holding two trench lines just 250 yards away – in a determined attack the Guards took both trenches, killing nearly all of the defenders.

The attack was quickly reorganised and they jumped off from the captured trenches towards the original objective. On their left the 1st Guards Brigade had reached their objective but the 6th Division on their right had made no progress at all – and the battalion now took heavy casualties from concentrated machine gun fire from high ground to their right. Despite this the target trench was taken by assault – many of the defending Germans surrendering.

Most of the battalion's officers were casualties and the surviving men had gotten split up – some were mixed up with other units but a group of 63 Coldstreams under the

Adjutant were holding the captured position along with some lost troops from the Irish and Scots Guards. A party of 40 Coldstreams under a Lieutenant now joined them and they settled in to defend whilst under heavy fire from their right.

This party was completely isolated with both flanks exposed and after beating off two counter-attacks – in which their remaining officers became casualties – they were ordered to withdraw to the captured trenches behind them. Here they stayed in defence, organising and consolidating the position which was shelled and counter-attacked by the Germans but the attacks were broken up before they reached the trenches. Small parties from the 20th Division came up during the night to mount bombing attacks on the German positions.

Three battalions of the 20th came up around 3.00am on the 16th and lay out in front of the trench line under enemy fire until 9.30am when they went forward to attack and take a portion of the enemy trench.

During the night of the 16th, the 1st Coldstreams were relieved and marched to a bivouac five miles to the rear. They had entered battle the previous morning with 17 officers and 690 other ranks and now paraded just two unwounded officers and 221 other ranks. One of the 484 men lost by the battalion on the 15th September was John Miles – he has no known grave and is remembered on the Somme's Thiepval Memorial.

John had spent just 101 days in France.

John's effects were valued at £5.6s.7d which was paid to his father on 22nd February 1917, who also later received a War Gratuity for John's service, a sum of £4 paid on 20 September 1919.

Major (Rtd) Mick McCarthy reads the eulogy for Charles Miles, Royal Warwickshire Regt

11th September 2016. Over 140 villagers and regimental representatives turned out to attend the Centenary Memorial Parade, wreath laying at the War Memorial and service on The Common as Holmer Green paid tribute to three of its Heroes, 100 years after they fell on the Somme.

CHAPTER 8

John Edward Palmer and Edwin Ephraim Palmer

John and Ephraim were the fourth and seventh children from the marriage of Charles Owen Slade Palmer (known as Owen) and Susan Johnson – who had fourteen children in all. Owen had been born in the nearby village of Coleshill and his family had lived round and about the area for at least two centuries – in Amersham, Beaconsfield and Wycombe.

Owen married Susan in September 1885 and they settled down in her home village of Stokenchurch and started their family – to keep them, Owen was a woodturner in the local chair trade.

We mentioned their eldest son, Abel, in an earlier chapter as he married Minnie Miles in 1909 – Minnie was the sister of two more of our Holmer Green Heroes – Charles and John Miles – and also first cousin to Sidney and Horace Miles who are remembered on the Penn Street war memorial. Another of Owen and Susan's children, Sarah, also married into the Miles family although not until 1941 – her second husband was Henry Miles, a brother to Charles, John and Minnie. Sarah's first husband was William Wright who she'd married in 1909.

John Edward Palmer was born on 9th May 1890, the family was still in Stokenchurch then but later moved to Terriers on the outskirts of Wycombe and then to Holmer Green around 1905. John later moved in with his sister Sarah and her husband William Wright. John then met and married Florence, neé King, always known as Flossie, in April 1915. Flossie already had a son called Reginald who had been born in 1910 and John and Flossie then had Charles who was born in April 1916 and John who was born in early 1919.

Charles and Susan Palmer at Rose Villa, Parish Piece, parents to John Edward Palmer and Edwin Ephraim Palmer.

John Palmer.

John and Flossie Palmer with baby Charles and Reginald 1916.

Flossie King 1916.

John does not appear to have been called up until quite late in the war – around the middle of 1918. He was an agricultural labourer before the war and may have been in a protected occupation or his health may have been poor and he wasn't fit to serve before then. Either way, after basic training he was posted to the Royal Army Service Corps in France but within a few months was on his way back to England having been given contaminated water to drink. He was sent to a temporary Military Hospital which had been set up in Carrington Council School in Nottingham where he spent the winter of 1918/1919. This was a time of a major influenza out-break known as Spanish Flu and it took the lives of many millions of people across the world. John's death certificate notes that he had influenza for seven days and pneumonia for three and a half days, dying on 16th March 1919 aged 28.

John's wife, Flossie, was paid £10.17s.9d on 28th July 1919 for the value of his effects and including a War Gratuity of £5.00. John is buried here in the village in the Christ Church graveyard – he was laid to rest in the grave of his baby sister, Marjorie, who had died on 20th October

1906, aged just two and a half years. John's memorial stone was erected by Flossie and remembers Marjorie on one side of the plinth and Ephraim Palmer on the other side – although if you visit the grave you may note that the inscription for Ephraim incorrectly reads Edward Ephraim.

Although baptised as Edwin Ephraim Palmer following his birth in January 1897, he was known all of his life as Ephraim. In 1911 he was 14 and living at home with his parents and six younger siblings. He was already learning his father's trade and was an apprentice chair leg turner.

Ephraim enlisted at High Wycombe around November 1915 and was posted to the King's Royal Rifle Corps in the 16th Battalion which had recently landed at Le Havre as part of the 100th Brigade in the 33rd Division for service on the Western Front.

He was then posted to the 10th Battalion of the same regiment which saw action at the Battle of Mont Sorrel in June 1916, the Battle of Delville Wood in July 1916 and the Battle of Guillemont in September 1916 as well as the Battle of Flers–Courcelette in September 1916, the Battle

Rose Villas, the Palmers' house in Parish Piece where John and Ephraim lived, pictured in 1961.

of Morval in September 1916 and the Battle of Le Transloy in October 1916 before taking part in the advance to the Hindenburg Line, the Battle of Langemarck in August 1917, the Battle of the Menin Road Ridge in September 1917, the Battle of Polygon Wood in September 1917 and the Battle of Cambrai in November 1917. At some point, he was transferred to the regiment's 11th Battalion but as the 10th and 11th were in the same brigade they took part in the same campaigns.

The 11th's duties thereafter became more of holding sections of the line in a cycle of being up in the front line, in billets for rest and training, in the support trenches and then back into the front line. The winter and spring of early 1918 was spent on the Somme sector, later moving to the Pas-de-Calais area and then to a position roughly half way between Arras and Cambrai. The casualty reports

	NAME AND SURNAME	RELATIONSHIP to Head of Family.	AGE		PARTICULARS as to MARRIAGE				PROFESSION or OCCUPATION				BIRTHPLACE	NATIONALITY	INFIRMITY
1	Charles Owen Palmer	Head	46		Married	25				Farm Labourer	148		Worker	Coleshill Hertfordshire	310
2	Susan Palmer	Wife		43	Married		14	12	2	Beads Work	875			Stoke Mandeville Bucks	
3	Ephraim Palmer	Son	14							Apprentice Chairwood Turner			Worker	Holmer Green Bucks	
4	Susan Palmer	Daughter		12						School	360			Terriers Bucks	
5	Ivy Palmer	Daughter		10										Terriers Bucks	
6	Owen Palmer	Son	7											Terriers Bucks	
7	Albert Palmer	Son	5											Holmer Green	
8	Sidney Palmer	Son	2											Holmer Green	
9	Stanley Palmer	Son	1											Holmer Green	

The Palmer family in the 1911 Census

Christ Church Holmer Green. Last resting place of John Edward Palmer, his brother Edwin Ephraim Palmer is also commemorated on the grave stone although buried in France

show a steady loss of men killed and wounded each week that they were in the front line – mainly from artillery fire and trench mortars.

In early September 1918 the battalion went into Divisional Reserve behind the lines for rest and reinforcement – moving back to the front line near Langemarck on 18th September where they immediately sustained some heavy losses from concentrated shell fire. On the night of the 19th they formed up in three waves and at 5.40am on the 20th launched an attack on Eagle Trench – however, the position was held by a considerable force of Germans with many machine guns and the attackers went to ground about 50 metres short of their objective. They went forward again but were stopped 10 metres before the trench with heavy losses. Two more attempts to carry the trench were made but without success, the survivors took shelter in shell-holes until nightfall. To their left, the attacking units had more success, capturing a length of Eagle Trench and consolidating the position, albeit with only 18 men initially fit to defend it. This position became a rally point for the men in the shell-holes and eventually some 90 men were in the captured part of Eagle Trench. At 11.00pm on the 20th, the remnants of the battalion were withdrawn, establishing themselves on the west bank of the Steenbeek river. They'd lost 6 officers killed and 3 wounded, 36 other ranks killed plus 43 missing and 127 wounded.

Ephraim Palmer was almost certainly one of the men wounded in this action. He is recorded as dying of his wounds on 4th October 1918. He was 21 years old and is buried in Houchin British Cemetery

Ephraim's Mother, Susan, was paid £32.10s.0d on 3rd May 1919 for the value of his effects and including a War Gratuity of £17.00.

CHAPTER 9
Ernest and Harold Salter

Frederick Salter c1875

The Salter family have been living around the area since at least the mid 1600s – the earliest that we have on record was John Salter who was born in Amersham in 1650. His children and grand-children were also recorded as being from Amersham, but one of his Grandsons, Charles, married a Chesham girl, Mary Ann Joiner (known as Ann), and they set up home in Holmer Green. Charles was born in Amersham in July 1818, Ann was slightly older having been born in January 1812 but by 1841 they were farming at Langley farm on the edge of Holmer Green where they lived with their five children. By 1851 Charles had fallen on hard times; the family were living in a cottage at Beamond End where Charles was now an agricultural labourer and his wife was making lace to supplement the family income.

Another son, Frederick, was born in this year bringing the number of children to eight. A ninth, Fanny, would be born in the following year to complete the family. Against the odds Frederick, or Fred as he was known, grew up to be a successful businessman. He married Sarah Bunce – a Great Kingshill girl – on 2nd June 1873 and together they also had nine children.

In 1881, Fred had a greengrocers in Islington where they were living with their first five children which included Ernest who had been born in late 1879. Ten years later and they were based in Paddington, still a greengrocer at 17 Kersal Road and with eight children at home.

Langley Farm, this building c.1820s replaced a much earlier farm house. It appears isolated now but prior to enclosure was served by a trackway from the dip in Watchet Lane to the centre of the village, the double-hedged track is still visible today.

Fred maintained his Buckinghamshire links throughout and by the turn of the century he had built a large house in Holmer Green called 'Woodlands' in Hunts Road – now Earl Howe Road – which has been replaced by a cul-de-sac, and another house called 'Woodville' on the corner of Hunts Road and Factory Street (now Orchard Way), this still survives. The 1901 census records Fred and Sarah living at Salters Folly, No 1 Hunts Road, with Ruth, Arthur and now Harold who had been born in 1894 to complete the family.

Fred acquired land and planted a substantial acreage of orchards adjoining Hunts Road and Factory Street and along Brown's Road. His sons John, William and Arthur helped Fred in what had become a considerable commercial concern. John, the eldest of Fred's children, married Ellen Craske on 20th February 1896 and by 1901 had his own greengrocers shop at 82 Shepherds Bush Road, Hammersmith.

Fruit, especially cherries, had been an important crop in the village for over 200 years, but Fred Salter brought its marketing to a new height of professionalism. He still had his own greengrocers shop in London, selling both his own fruit and that purchased from local growers.

Woodville, Orchard Way, built by Fred Salter.

Woodlands Close, built on the site of Salter's house, Woodland.

John Salter's London greengrocers shop.

Beamond End.

The shop was being run by Fred's third son, also called Frederick, who was now married – and they had the 21 year old Ernest with them who was likewise working in the family business. By 1911 though John and his family were back in the local area, living at Beamond End and working at Beamond End Farm where his father, Fred, now lived and farmed.

Fred Salter specialised in unusual fruit on which he became an expert – two local delicacies were Bullace, a small plum, and Medlars, best eaten when rotten. In 1892, a deep interest in apples had led Fred to Steeple Aston in Oxfordshire. This small, stone built Cotswold village boasted a host of orchards filled with fruit from one end of the village to the other. The profusion of fruit was such that the villagers did not know what to do with it all. Reports of this glut of Bramleys, Worcesters, Blenheims, Wellingtons and Russets had somehow reached Fred's ears and he set out in the following May to make the locals an offer.

Fred alighted from the train at Heyford station, walked up the hill and made a slow perambulation of the village, paying attention to the valley that was a mass of pink and white blossom. He took every opportunity to talk to the friendly locals, especially the orchard owners, and invited them to meet with him in the White Lion

Bullace.

Inn that evening. Fred was there early and had ordered bread and cheese (fourpence) and a glass of beer (twopence) and waited for his guests in front of a blazing log fire. Before long, with drinks all-round, Fred was addressing his new-found Oxfordshire friends and offered them a deal. He would pay for the blossom, which in several cases paid for the entire year's rent on their cottages. The title to all the apples would then be his. This was a gamble, he had to rely on the honesty of the villagers and that a late frost would not destroy the crop. This scheme was known as 'buying the blossom'.

A good cherry crop.

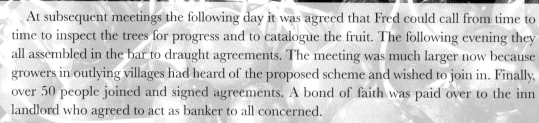

At subsequent meetings the following day it was agreed that Fred could call from time to time to inspect the trees for progress and to catalogue the fruit. The following evening they all assembled in the bar to draught agreements. The meeting was much larger now because growers in outlying villages had heard of the proposed scheme and wished to join in. Finally, over 50 people joined and signed agreements. A bond of faith was paid over to the inn landlord who agreed to act as banker to all concerned.

There was no late frost that year, the evenings grew longer, the sun poured down on the trees giving abundance and beauty to the apple crop. During August Fred arrived at the village driving a horse and van and accompanied by his son William, then almost 18 years old. The journey had taken two whole days to travel from his London shop to Steeple Aston, staying at the 'Gravel Diggers Arms' on the Oxford road. It was arranged that William should stay at the inn until the crops had been gathered and dispatched to London.

This is a remarkable story of 'rags to riches' achieved by Fred Salter and his family within quite a short time, an entrepreneurial spirit that helped put the 'Great' into Great Britain.

In March 1902 Ernest Salter married Elizabeth Smith in Kensington and the 1911 census shows them set up as greengrocers at 196 Westbourne Grove in Paddington – the shop still exists today although no longer a greengrocers. We have almost no details of Ernest's war service as his records did not survive the WWII blitz. He enlisted in Kensington, near his home, but whether as a volunteer earlier in the war or as a conscript later on we don't know. The only definite record we have is of him being in the Royal Engineers, rated as a Driver, and serving at the Haynes Park Signal Depot in Bedfordshire, England at the time of his death. We lack any information as to whether he had already served overseas and was back in the UK for further training or recuperating from injuries or whether this had been his base since completing basic training.

Haynes Park Signal Depot in Bedfordshire.

On the 17th October 1917, Ernest took his own life – the Deputy Coroner for the County of Bedfordshire recorded the cause of death as: 'Injuries caused by cutting his throat with a razor whilst he was temporarily insane'. He is buried in the churchyard of St Mary's Church in Haynes Park – with a view right across the grounds of the country estate where the Signal Depot was established. He has a beautiful memorial, erected by Elizabeth and engraved with a line taken from a popular funeral hymn of the time – "Sleep on dear one and take your rest".

The Army record of Ernest's List of Effects survives but although it shows a total value of £5.6s.11d there is no record of them paying that amount to his widow. Nor did Elizabeth receive a War Gratuity for her loss – the record simply notes 'suicide. Not admissible.' However, after probate completed on 25 January 1918 his estate was valued at £304.14s.0d and was left to Elizabeth Salter, widow, of 196 Westbourne Grove.

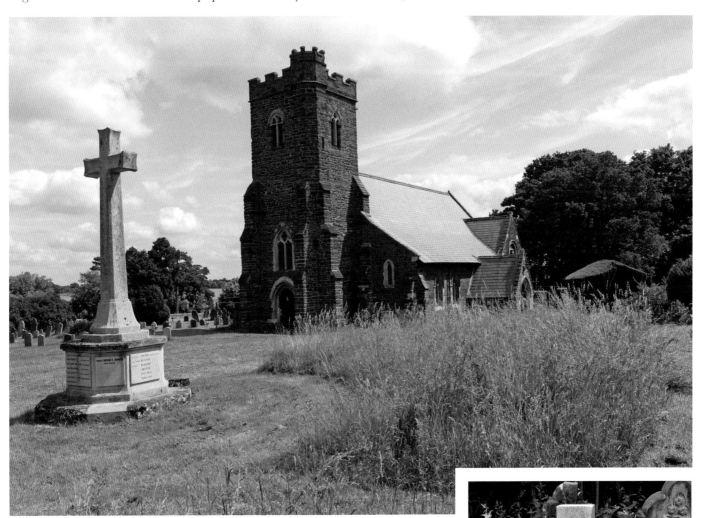

Ernest Salter's last resting place in the churchyard of St Mary's Church in Haynes Park cemetery, Bedfordshire.

Ernest Salter's Holmer Green Heroes wreath laid at Haynes Park cemetery, Bedfordshire.

Meanwhile, Harold Salter had also gone into the family business – the 1911 census tells us that the 16 year old Harold was working in the greengrocers being run by his elder brother William – Fred and Sarah's second child – at 31 Richmond Road, Hammersmith. Harold enlisted around February 1916, a few months before his 22nd birthday. He was posted to the 2/16th Battalion of the London Regiment – the Queen's Own Westminster Rifles. With them he was to see some very varied active service.

They embarked for France on 22nd June 1916, going into the line at Neuville St Vaast. It was a relatively quiet sector and the only offensive action they engaged in was a successful raid into the enemy trenches during September. On 24th October they were relieved and marched to the Somme area but were diverted and made their way to the port of Marseille. Here they embarked on 17th November and sailed to Salonica, disembarking there on the 30th and then moving on to Thessaly to take up positions guarding two mountain passes. However, no fighting took place and the threat having dissipated by February they marched back across Greece to Bulgaria, taking up positions on the Vardar front on 18th March and taking part in several minor operations which included the capture by the Battalion of Goldies Hill on 8th May and holding it against repeated counter attacks.

On 21st June 1917 the Battalion was transferred to the Egyptian Expeditionary Force and embarked for Alexandria, arriving on the 25th. Through marches and on trains they made their way across Egypt towards Palestine but engaged in no military actions. Instead they were able to spend three months training and preparing before playing a part in the offensive against the Turks around Beersheba which started on 17th October. They were involved in much of the fighting as the EEF pushed north and forced the enemy evacuation of Jerusalem which the EEF entered on 9th December 1917.

Harold Salter: Seen here stacking tennis racket frames as part of the drying process, note others hanging from the orchard trees. Harold was at this time employed by tennis racket manufacturer William Dean working in New Pond Road.

The Queen's Westminster Rifles initially went into defensive positions north of Jerusalem and sustained the brunt of several enemy attacks until the EEF was able to push on again in a series of attacks which led to the occupation of Jericho. The Battalion took part in a major raid on 22nd March 1918 which forced a crossing of the River Jordan and did much damage to railway and communication networks before withdrawing back to their lines – a later, second assault in late April eventually had to be abandoned after four days of fighting as the enemy had heavily reinforced.

The Division that the Queen's had been part of was now dissolved and the Battalion was posted back to France, making their way back across Egypt to Alexandria where they detrained on 16th June and were immediately embarked the same day onto H.M.T Indarra. However it didn't sail until 18th June and what conditions were like sealed up on board a ship in Alexandria harbour in mid June can only be imagined.

Three days later at 4.00am on 21st June the Indarra was attacked by a German submarine but fortunately escaped damage, arriving at Taranto harbour on the heel of Italy on the afternoon of the same day. After a couple of days in camp here they entrained for France, leaving at 11.00pm on the 24th and rejoining the British Expeditionary Force at Moulle in France seven days later on 1st July 1918.

July and August passed relatively uneventfully (for a front line unit on the Western Front) with the Battalion alternately moving up to the front around Moth Farm or in billets back from the line at St. Sylvestre. September started the same way with the Queen's in reserve trenches on the 1st, moving forward on the 2nd, in support to another battalion of the London Regiment on the 3rd and 4th and then taking over the front line trenches on the 5th September. Here they stayed until the 8th when they were relieved back to billets.

Harold Salter's death is a mystery. He is recorded as being killed in action on 6th September 1918 but the unit war diary only records the loss of two Other Ranks wounded on that day. It notes that the Battalion was holding the front line and they had patrols out who would observe and harass the enemy. There is no record of either of the wounded men dying from their injuries but in any case, if Harold had been one of them his death should have been recorded as died from wounds. His medal record card clearly shows his travels with the Battalion to all the above countries and battles but exactly how he died remains unknown.

What is certain is that he is buried in Mont Noir Cemetery, a small cemetery near the top of a steep slope which was part of the front line at this time. There are a number of French graves here together with the British graves and most of these men will have fallen very close to this spot. You can't drive up to the cemetery, it is accessible only by climbing up a bridle path from the lower road.

Harold's Register of Effects showed his effects were valued at £17.15s.7d although the Regiment deducted 9s.7d for some unspecified recharge. The remainder was split between his mother, Sarah, and his sister Annie – now Annie Wickson having married John Wickson in 1909 – each received £8.13s.0d on 9th August 1919, over a year after his death. The War Gratuity of £12.10s.0d was also divided between these two ladies, each receiving £6.5s.0d on 7th July 1920.

Mont Noir Cemetery, resting place of Harold Salter.

Holmer Green

Cuckoo Town

WATCHET LANE

Allotments

HEATH END ROAD

BEECHTREE ROAD

BEECHTREE ROAD

RECREAT

Recrea
Groun

HAZELS LANE

TWO HEDGES

WORK HOUSE HILL

RECREATION DRI

WATCHET LANE

PARISH PIECE

BOTTOM ALLEY

HUNTS ROAD

FACTORY STREET

THE ALLEY

FOX RD.

FEAT

VILLAGE MAP

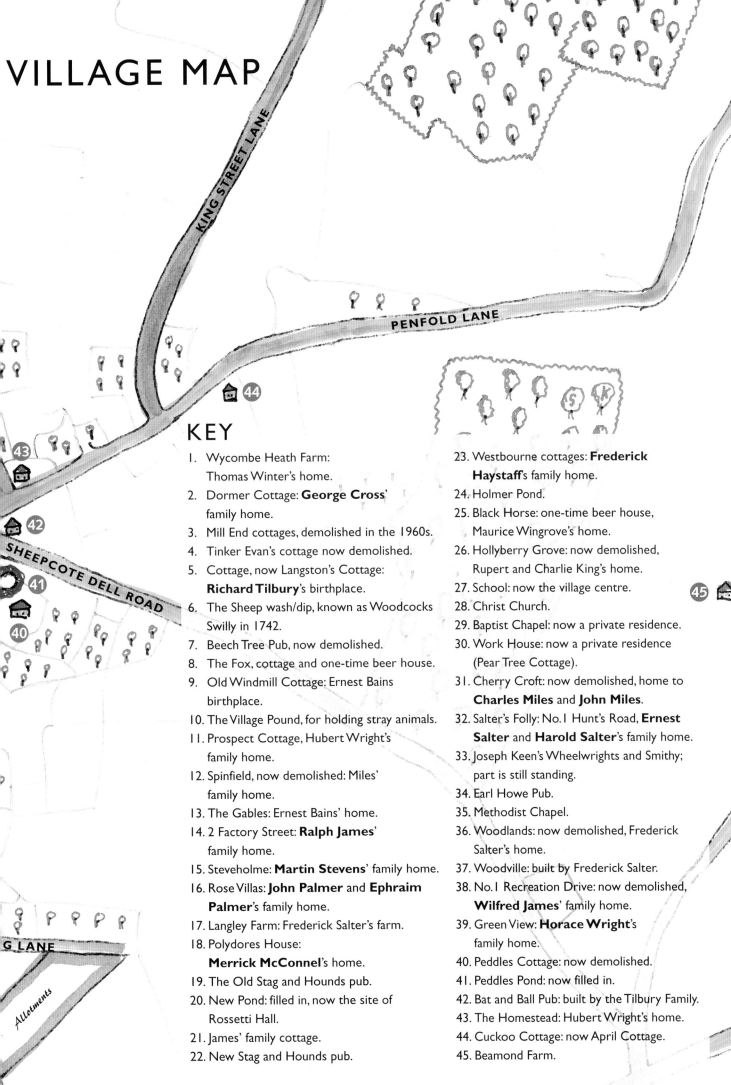

KEY

1. Wycombe Heath Farm: Thomas Winter's home.
2. Dormer Cottage: **George Cross'** family home.
3. Mill End cottages, demolished in the 1960s.
4. Tinker Evan's cottage now demolished.
5. Cottage, now Langston's Cottage: **Richard Tilbury**'s birthplace.
6. The Sheep wash/dip, known as Woodcocks Swilly in 1742.
7. Beech Tree Pub, now demolished.
8. The Fox, cottage and one-time beer house.
9. Old Windmill Cottage: Ernest Bains birthplace.
10. The Village Pound, for holding stray animals.
11. Prospect Cottage, Hubert Wright's family home.
12. Spinfield, now demolished: Miles' family home.
13. The Gables: Ernest Bains' home.
14. 2 Factory Street: **Ralph James'** family home.
15. Steveholme: **Martin Stevens'** family home.
16. Rose Villas: **John Palmer** and **Ephraim Palmer**'s family home.
17. Langley Farm: Frederick Salter's farm.
18. Polydores House: **Merrick McConnel**'s home.
19. The Old Stag and Hounds pub.
20. New Pond: filled in, now the site of Rossetti Hall.
21. James' family cottage.
22. New Stag and Hounds pub.
23. Westbourne cottages: **Frederick Haystaff**'s family home.
24. Holmer Pond.
25. Black Horse: one-time beer house, Maurice Wingrove's home.
26. Hollyberry Grove: now demolished, Rupert and Charlie King's home.
27. School: now the village centre.
28. Christ Church.
29. Baptist Chapel: now a private residence.
30. Work House: now a private residence (Pear Tree Cottage).
31. Cherry Croft: now demolished, home to **Charles Miles** and **John Miles**.
32. Salter's Folly: No.1 Hunt's Road, **Ernest Salter** and **Harold Salter**'s family home.
33. Joseph Keen's Wheelwrights and Smithy; part is still standing.
34. Earl Howe Pub.
35. Methodist Chapel.
36. Woodlands: now demolished, Frederick Salter's home.
37. Woodville: built by Frederick Salter.
38. No.1 Recreation Drive: now demolished, **Wilfred James'** family home.
39. Green View: **Horace Wright**'s family home.
40. Peddles Cottage: now demolished.
41. Peddles Pond: now filled in.
42. Bat and Ball Pub: built by the Tilbury Family.
43. The Homestead: Hubert Wright's home.
44. Cuckoo Cottage: now April Cottage.
45. Beamond Farm.

Among the cherries

It seems fitting to look at the fruit growing history of our village here, and orchards have a long pedigree in Holmer Green as can be clearly seen on the 1742 Map of the Manor of Holmer. At first glance it might be thought that this windswept Chiltern hill-top community would be completely unsuitable, too unhospitable for such a crop, in fact fruit thrives here, it maybe has something to do with our clay ridden soil. We are not alone, nearby hill-top settlements have a similar history such as Little Kingshill, Prestwood, Weston Turvill, Seer Green and Flackwell Heath among others.

Cherries were the main crop although some apples, pears and specialist varieties were grown. By the end of the 19th century some locals were also growing soft fruit such as gooseberries, raspberries and black/red currents. Children would take time out of school to help with the picking, as they would also help with the general harvest-time activities and stone picking in the autumn – all to earn a few extra pennies or provide free labour on the family farm.

Picking fruit in the orchards was a different situation, tall ladders were involved. These required good arm muscles and balance to manoeuvre, along with a light touch when removing cherries complete with their stalks without bruising them. A cherry picker also needed to

work quickly as he (it was always a he) was paid by weight. Birds have always presented a problem and so a boy, a 'birdscarer' or 'bird-minder' was employed to rattle a tin can filled with stones, or to whirl a football rattle. Sometimes this lad would be trusted with a 'black-powder' gun, often of blunderbuss type. Pigeons and starlings were the main culprits and many a starling pie was enjoyed in the village.

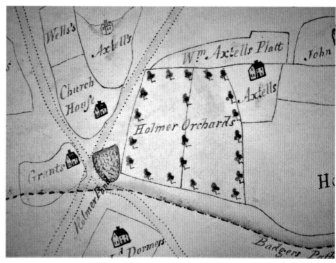

Detail from the 1742 map of the Manor of Holmer, note Holmer Pond by the cross roads (tracks).

Chiltern's Orchard, also known as Skimmer's Orchard abutting the 'Mile Straight' (A404) c1963.

Fruit was packed into willow sieves and most were taken to Great Missenden or Amersham railway station to be sold at the Covent Garden market early next morning, (local and fresh produce!)

This was seasonal work with the men deserting their regular employment. Many were local chair turners or chair makers, self-employed or employed – it was part of the accepted tradition of the place. In a good (fruit) year these men could earn substantially above their weekly income whilst enjoying a certain camaraderie amongst mates, this was even more so when 'fruiting up-country'.

Eight cherry trees planted along Earl Howe Road in 2008 to mark the first mention of the settlement of Holeme, eight hundred years before.

Holmer Green cherry picking gang.

Note the bird scarer, to his right is Nimmy Tyler

Nimmy Tyler's cottage in Penfold Lane – now Rosemary Cottage

Fruit picking up-country involved traveling to other fruit growing areas to chase the 'later fruit', these being apples, pears and prunes. Middle Green, Harmondsworth, Iver, Croxley Green and Western Turvill were typical destinations and these fruits ripened later than cherries and so provided an extended harvesting period. In most cases these weeks away from their families provided the only holiday these men would have all year.

Many farming communities held harvest home suppers, usually in a local farmer's barn to celebrate the gathering in of the last cut of corn, all paid for by the farmer – and no shortage of beer. To celebrate a successful cherry harvest, we in Holmer Green held our cherry pie Sunday, hosted by the Baptist Chapel on the common. The women folk would make up the pies, in the shape of a pasty, sometimes called a cherry bumper.

These confectioneries were filled with 'little blacks', the juicy wild cherries that grew in the medieval hedgerows so common to our village. Because so many were needed to satisfy the craving of local children many pie makers turned to local baker Fred Tucker to do the cooking, in true community spirit he obliged. The joy of the children eating their cherry pies with the purple juice running down their arms was a joy to behold and a special day of the year.

Harry Wingrove's orchard in Watchet Lane, cleared in the 1960s to create Harries Way and Fox Road.

Holmer Green families celebrate the cherry harvest.

Cherries in a cottage garden in Watchet Lane.

CHAPTER 10
Martin Stevens

The Stevens family have lived around the area for many generations. The earliest record we have traced shows that in 1765, Benjamin Stevens' wife Mary gave birth to William Stevens in Chalfont St Giles. William married Deborah Dodd from Farnham Royal in June 1791 and they had six boys and one girl together. The fifth child was Joseph born in 1800 who married Alice Jane Hall and they had ten children, the fourth of these being Arthur in March 1826 who was born in Widmer End, as were all of Joseph's children. Around the late 1840s, Joseph moved his family to become a farmer at the Wycombe Heath end of Holmer Green. However, despite this move, in 1852 Arthur married a Hughenden girl called Martha Lacey and they had eight children.

Arthur established his home in Holmer Green and the 1861 and 1871 census both record his occupation as Timber Dealer and Publican – this was of the New Stag & Hounds (now Turners Place) which he took over in 1860 and ran until 1890, even after the death of Martha in 1876.

Arthur and Martha's eldest was George who was born in 1853. George became a chair leg turner and in 1878 he married local girl Mary Ann Eustace. They set up home in The Alley (now Pond Approach) where Mary gave birth to seven children, the two youngest being Ralph on 1st May 1888 and Martin who was born in October 1890. In later years George also acted as the Parish Constable for the village.

Ralph initially became a stockman, working with the animals on a local farm but by his early twenties he was a chair back maker working with his father who was still turning chair legs in their cottage. Martin too became a chair leg turner like his father.

Ralph married Daisy Langston of Great Kingshill on 29 December 1915 – and Daisy's sister, Mabel, married Ralph's cousin, Eli Stevens. Ralph and Daisy had three children, the first of which, Doris, was born during the war in December 1916 and was often mentioned in Ralph and Daisy's letters to each other after he was called up in early January 1917. Ralph went into the Royal Artillery, initially with 23rd Reserve Battery at Boyton Camp in Wiltshire. He was posted to France in May 1917 with the 8th Royal Artillery Division but had lots of trouble with his feet (possibly trench foot) and by October 1917 he was no longer Gunner Stevens but was now Private Stevens with the Labour Corps, working out of 173 Labour Camp. Men who were no longer fit enough to remain with active service battalions through poor health or wounds, continued to serve in the front line in the Labour Corps. They dug new trenches and repaired damaged ones, dug drainage systems, repaired roads and bridges – whatever was needed to keep the army in the front line – and frequently under fire themselves.

Martin received his call up papers from a Mr H.E. Fellows on 19th April 1916 and was sent to Caterham in Surrey for training with the Coldstream Guards.

The New Stag and Hounds pub, Bottom Alley.

The Stevens family farmed at Primrose Farm, image dated c late 19th century.
L-R standing; Eli, Fred and William Stevens L-R sitting; Eli's wife Alice with baby Richard (Dick) and Mother with baby Robert (Bob).

On 30th December 1916 he was posted to 2nd Battalion Coldstream Guards but was then posted to the 3rd Battalion in France on 18th January 1917. He was now part of the 3rd's No.1 Company and in No.1 Platoon.

The Coldstreams were frequently in action throughout 1917 and into early 1918 – First and Second Battles of the Scarpe, Battle of Arleux, Battle of Cambrai, Battle of St Quentin, Battle of Bapaume, First Battle of Arras, Battle of Estaires, Battle of Hazebrouck and then the Defence of Nieppe Forest during the great German Spring Offensive

Primrose Farm, Primrose Hill, ancestral home to the Stevens Family. In the 19th century it was also a pub called the Forresters Arms.

The Stevens letters

The following are extracts from over 40 letters mostly written by Martin and Ralph Stevens, many from the battlefield, with others from relations and friends. These letters can only convey a little of the emotion, trauma and life changing events that were unfolding on the other side of the English Channel, family life would never be the same in Holmer Green. Many of these letters are written on YMCA headed paper. This organisation (founded in c1844) built thousands of wooden huts all over England and the Continent to provide comfort for servicemen passing through on their way to war. Apart from providing food, entertainment and the opportunity for Christian worship the YMCA also provided free writing materials. Holmer Green resident Thomas Winter (see elsewhere) was prominent in the YMCA during WW1. The letters are transcribed verbatim and include the writer's spelling and grammar and sometimes names and locations had been censored.

Ralph Stevens

"My Dear Mother & Dad

I thought I would just drop you a line & let you know how I was fairing as I expect you have heard by now where I was it was about the last of my thoughts to land in the R A they didn't examine me any more at Oxford they put me into the Artillery strait away I have had my papers today & I see I am a Gunner but I don't know my address at present but will let me old Dais have it as soon as I can I didn't half think of home last night when very tired had to kip down on the boards I had no sleep I can tell you it was so cold in the bargain but I suppose we shall get used to it. It makes you think about the others that have been through it for us. I must say that today we have had a very good living although it is in a tough way but plenty of it so must not grumble Well Dears I think I have told you as much as I know of the army at present so will change the subject with much love from your loving Son Ralph"

18330 M Stevens No 1 Company, 3rd Battalion Coldstream Gds, Guards Division, B.E.F France – January 22nd 1917

The Stevens family chair bodging in Parish Piece.
L-R; George snr, George, brother to Martin seated on the shave horse

"My Dear Father & Mother

You will be wondering how I am getting on, well I am fine & trust you are all same at home, I am often thinking of you all & wondering how you are getting on, I have had no letters since leaving England. You will notice that I have been transferred to the 3rd Battalion from the 2nd Batt, so please don't make this mistake and put the 2nd as I shall have to wait a long time before I get any news from you.

You will send on Ralphs address when next you write, shall then be able to write to him, have heard nothing of him....?...., Freddy Darvill & Earnest Pearce were telling me that he was stationed at ....?......, they had heard from home they were both looking well, only saw them twice although they were there the whole of the time, and they said they had not seen Fred while there, they had heard that I was out so of course were looking for me each time the Guards passed.

Martin Stevens

Young Martin Stevens with Lucy the cow

"My Dear Father & Mother

I think it is your turn to have a letter Well Dears I hope you are both well as it leaves me well. I have had a bad cold but is much better it is a very dull place here but I have been to Chapel this morning there is only one little place here about 2 minutes away our hut & as soon as I got there & heard the old Sankeys Hymns it made it seem a little more like home we had a very nice address from the Chaplain & the first Hymn we had was Jesus Saviour Pilot one & then we had I need thee every hour & then we had when the soul? Os called up yonder I'll be there & I didn't to let into the tenor part it seemed nice to have a sing at these old Hymns in the afternoon I went to a

Cpl. J. MASON'S Squad, Coldstream Guards, May, 1916.

Pvt Martin Stevens with his unit – enlarged detail below.

bible Class in the School in the Afternoon there were about 40 or 50 of us & one of the young men in my hut gave the address then When the class was over they got us a nice tea at the Charge of 4d each & then after tea we had solos & etc. till six I quite enjoyed it , was a very nice tea it is a farmer & his wife & daughters who provide the tea so we had some nice fresh butter which very nice I tell you & then at six o clock we went to Chapel & came out at ¼ Past ? & then went to the Salvation Army hut & had some more singing & Address from Soldiers So I consider I made the best of the Sunday I would have much rather been at home with you all but cannot so must make this life as bright as we can, I hope & trust it won't be for long I hope & pray this terrible war will soon be over. Ada tells me that Mr Darvill is Dead I am sorry Poor old Chap I wonder how they will go on it will make it bad for bert? & Mrs Darvill as he told them something before he went away. Well Dears I think I will close this as I have got to be off to gun drill again we have it a bit stiff now Kindly remember me to My Dear old Dais I shall write to her tomorrow if I have time hope you will understand this I have wrote it in a hurry

I Remain your loving Son Ralph xxxxxxx"

"This is a rough miserable looking place, they seem to be doing very little with this land, the old Farmers where we are staying does his work with the help of his wife & two daughters they have been thrashing with the old flails yesterday & today they are cleaning, they would have smiled had I had a go at it with them wouldn't they but my strokes might have been longer than the old Gentleman & so caught him on his napper so perhaps it's as well that I left it to them.

Tell Aunt Alice I wrote to Fred when at his base, had no reply before leaving so do not know his whereabouts, perhaps she would give you his address to send on to me, I trust they are keeping well all of them, please give them my love, also all my old friends at H.G. have you had James home as yet, now with much love to all Brothers & Sisters I close,

Ever your loving Son, xxxxxMartinxx"

Mary Stevens aged 20

"My Dear Dad & Mum

A Parcel from Flo was waiting for us on return from the line this time last night I have not received yours as yet but may do so yet, I'm hoping so anyway, I quite understand how you managed to get it as you did.

Some of the news I was very sorry to hear, especially of poor Will Keen. One would have thought to look at him that he had the best of health & would live as long as he liked as the saying goes, I'm sorry for his wife being one who is not strongest herself but her family is growing up now & they have a little to go on with its so nice to know that Amy has got on good terms again, it's a terrible thing when brothers & sisters cannot agree.

Well dears while writing this your parcel has arrived it was rather cracked but nevertheless the contents were quite eatable, & it cost me nothing, thank you so much for same".

Flo was Martin's girlfriend – courting since 1913. This is Flora Cope of Spurlands Farm – now Copes Farm (above).
William Keen was the village wheelwright who died March 1917 aged 46. His daughter, Edith Elsie, born 1910 later married Martin's brother George's son, Wilfred.

The Steven's family home, Steveholme, situated on the corner of Pond Approach and Parish Piece. Note the outbuilding- the 'wood house' for storing fire wood, often pronounced the 'ood us' in local dialect.

"My Dear Father & Mother

Many thanks for parcel arrived on this twenty sixth it arrived in good fresh condition, the contents were just what I was longing for the pies was lovely, went down good for supper, you could not send a better, oxo cubes I am not very fond of.

So pleased to hear that all at home were well also to be able to say that I am bonnie, we are having a rest now again, hope this mud will have dried up a bit before we go in again, we had a good time, but for that last trip.

I must now tell you I have been very fortunate getting parcels this month, from Flo, Ada, Aunt Carrie, Miss Kingdon & yours, they were very handy too, we are now able to get a few little things so you need not send for some time now again I will write & let you know when running short.

Where has brother Ralph got to, have not heard from him for some time, nor from Cousin Fred I trust they are both well, how are you getting on with the gardening & etc. I hope you will manage to get it all done as it will come in next winter very useful, there will be a scarcity of things then & we lads shall want a lot then you know.

How are Mrs Keen & family getting on it's a pity the boys are not old enough to carry on his little business, but it may be that they will do better in some other line, I don't think there was a great lot in it.

"My Dear Father & Mother

Yes I should very much love to join you on Sunday at the old Chappel, to listen to a few old hands would be very refreshing. Should also like to give you a call through the kitchen window at half past three as I used to do, that time may be soon, so will keep a cheerful courage on.

Ever your loving Son Martin xxx"

Martin's sister Ada

"My Dear Father & Mother

I am writing to you an extra letter this week for I have some good news to tell.

After tea yesterday I was stood at the door of the hut when a voice from behind said, Hullo old boy, I knew this voice, whipped around and there stood dear brother Ralph, I found him some tea after which we took a walk together, across to his camp which is hardly half an hours walk away from me, this evening we are meeting again & going to a service given by his Wesleyan Chaplain, he has been staying five weeks where he is, we came down this lane to this place a week ago, wish we had known this when first I arrived here still we may have many evenings together even now, he is looking well has good billets (not overdone with food) but has a nice little shop to work in, am so pleased he is on that work, he gets on well at it & all his mates like him (Steve they call him) he had received your photo of Daisy & baby, they are splendid I think & he is so pleased with them, he has also had Albert's letter & W Pursey's he will not be able to send you a photo of himself as there are no places here to get it done you must not expect many letters from him as they are limited to two per week, I will let you know when we either of us move, probably not for some time, I don't suppose I shall write so many letters now as we shall get out together all the spare time we have.

This weather is now grand out here as we were out practising this morn we went through a little Copse as used to be & it was full of violets cowslips & anemones (is that the way to spell it) & I had to say how lovely, did not think so much of them as I do now, when at home.

Now I must be off as I shall keep Ralphie waiting Trusting all at home are well love to all.

Ever your loving Son Martin xxxxxx"

Ralph Stevens aged 21

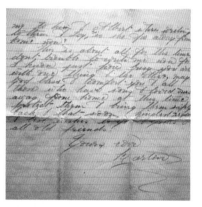

George Stevens outside the family home, Steveholme, brother to Martin (inset) and Ralph

"My Dear Father & Mother

How are you getting on, I hope well, pleased to say I am bonnie am now moved from Ralph, we are on fatigues, it's a lovely country where our tents are pitched. Fields of Lucerne & clover, have had some showers, which with the sunshine is pulling things along if you have weather similar at home its making up for some of the lost time, rather too good for work middle of day.

Well R & I had a splendid time during the fortnight we were together, was sorry to leave him , but it's good to know that he is so comfortably stationed & that he's safe & well. I had the pleasure of seeing his wife & little girl, they I think look fine I don't suppose we shall be home to help you with the fruit hay work & etc. am hoping to hear more good news after this conference, all seems to be going well with us just now cannot realise myself what it will be like when its all over, fancy its nearly thirteen month since I left you, quite a long holiday isn't it.

Had a letter from Flo this morning tells me she has been over to see you again, she says you were both well, aunt Lizzie was there, was sorry to hear Uncle Will was dead its been a funny life for her while he was alive, but I suppose she will miss him, & not know what to do with her time & self now it's a good thing she has the house bringing in a little, but I don't suppose its sufficient to keep her.

Then poor old Henry Brown has gone at last it will be a great relief to Miss Alice, & life had no pleasures for him this last few years, he has been bedridden for twenty years now I should think.

Henry Brown, retired farmer was in 1911 living at Holly Cottage (later the White House) aged 87 with wife Mary and 48 year old unmarried daughter Alice (pictured above).

Alice was to serve on the parish council for 40 years as Parish Clerk, Alice Close is named after her.

On 1st April 1918, Martin's battalion came out of the line and moved in stages to billets at Tincques, just west of Arras, arriving at 5.00pm on the 2nd. They stayed here until the 10th when they moved out of the camp at nightfall and spent the night waiting along a road side. At 11.00am the next morning a fleet of buses arrived and the whole Guards Brigade embussed, making their way to a position on the road between Strazeele and Estaires – to the south west of Ypres.

At 2.30am on 12th April the battalion went into the trenches – Martin's No.1 Company on the right front, No.3 Company centre, No.4 Company left front with No.2 Company in support. At day-break, the enemy opened up a heavy fire on the British trenches and at 8.00am, large numbers of the enemy were reported as advancing along the whole front. The Coldstreams repulsed the attack on their sector with rifle and machine gun fire but news was received that 50th Division had been driven back on their right so at 11.00am, No.1 Company attacked with 3 & 4 Companies conforming on their advance to straighten the line.

Martin Stevens' War Medals

Martin's Company met with a withering crossfire from German rifles and machine guns sited in ruined buildings and an orchard and were stopped after covering 400 yards. Here they held their ground till 3.00pm although only 40 men of all ranks were left, they then fell back to their original start position where it was realised that the 50th Division posts which had secured their flank had now disappeared.

The Germans attacked at 3.50pm, seeking to outflank No.1 Company who started to withdraw. No.2 Company came forward from support with elements of the Irish Guards and counter attacked the Germans, succeeding in restoring the original line and so No.1 held their position. At 4.20pm a heavy German barrage was followed by a strong infantry attack which was repulsed with heavy casualties. At dusk the Company withdrew to a support trench where rations and ammunition came up to them and they were able to spend a relatively quiet night.

At dawn an enemy armoured car came forward to give machine gun fire to the British forward posts and then at 6.30am an enemy attack developed which was successfully repulsed on the right but succeeded in penetrating between the centre and left Companies. The left Company fell back, leaving a gap which the 30 surviving men of No.1 Company attempted to fill. The Germans were now working around the flanks of the embattled Coldstreams whose situation was getting perilous.

The War Diary records in an unusually emotive form: "These boys held on until surrounded on three sides then attempted to fight their way back. Very few succeeded."

By the end of that day of the 13th April, the 3rd Coldstream Battalion were down to just 40 effectives. Private Martin Stevens was dead, killed by a sniper's shot to the head, almost certainly in that final stand when they were taking fire from three sides.

Martin's effects were valued at £8.6s.8d which was paid to his Father on 6th August 1918, George was also paid a War Gratuity of £9.00 on 12th December 1919.

A few weeks after Martin died, Flo Cope wrote to Martin's brother Ralph in France:

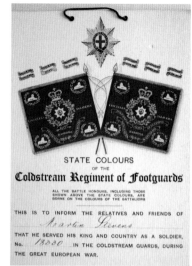

Martin's certificate of war service.

Dear Ralph

Thank you so much for your kind letter of a fortnight ago, have been going to answer so many times but somehow could not make a start.

Yes "Ralph" it was a sad blow, I can hardly bear it at times, & can hardly realize he will never come home again; I know all is well with him, it's we who are left to mourn for our loss; I am reminded of the words 'Ours the pain, but his, Oh his the undiminished gladness, the undecaying glory, the undeparted dream:" The sorrow is for those who love, and live on.

Dear old boy, his faith was so strong even in my last letters he was so looking forward to coming home to settle down; he told me he had had some rough journeys & what a comfort my prayers were, but asked me to pray more for the need grew greater every day but He Who had said my Grace is sufficient had always supplied that Grace & he also said He (Our Heavenly Father) would do that which was best for us both.

Well Ralph Its hard just now to think this is for the best & that as rich a love as ours should apparently be parted just now, Yet still I feel he is still mine only called to the Higher Service & we must believe it is best that he should serve in a Higher Grade than we since God willed it so.

I am glad he went off so quickly, for he had no time for regrets at leaving us all & no long suffering like some of the poor lads have.

I have had no letter from any of his mates which I feel is rather strange as I know Woodward had my address, I hope he is still safe, The Guards had a terrible time poor fellows & I am afraid we shall soon be having some more terrible news.

A cousin of mine was killed on the 10th. (three days before Martin) he was an only son & talented musician he was a favourite nephew of that cousin who Martin used to visit at Slough, I heard from her again yesterday, she is very grieved about both of them said they were the only two soldiers except her son (who is also in France) that she wrote to & they both went so close together.

I went to H Green on Monday & found all well, Doris grows a big girl now, I had a letter from Ada this morning & one of my letters to Martin returned there are three or four more somewhere.

Mrs White of Hambleden has only just received her husband's things from France & he died nine months ago I believe, my cousin says they have got young Wills already.

Now must close, I know you must feel this terribly Ralph & away there from all your dear ones it must be jolly hard, but I trust you may be spared to get home again & that soon.

With kindest regards from all at Spurlands & loving sympathy your Sincerely

Flo

PS I am hoping you may come across some of the Coldstream Grds at some time; or Fred may, now don't worry about me Ralph, God never gives a greater burden than we can bear, heavy as it may be:

I once told Martin we loved each other too much perhaps it was so, we had five happy years in spite of this war cloud, never had one unkind word to each other. I have many special memories.

My Dear Mother & Father

Well Dear Mother you asked me if I should be able to go & see Dear Martin's grave but unless we get moved there Dear as it is in a different section of the Front to what I am if I should get that way I would try & find it out you said Dear Mother how you would have liked to have seen the last of him & where he lies but I fear you wouldn't want to see the sights it would make you worse than ever. I can say he was taken in the best way as suffering, it's awful to be hit out by a shell some of the poor lads I have seen with most awful wounds so you have got that Consolation Dear Mother of knowing he didn't suffer & if he could but speak to us he would I feel shure say don't morn for me as I don't want to go back to that again & we all know that he is far better off, although we don't like loosing such a good Brother as he was but yet Dears we may yet live to see the working of it all,

Loving Son Ralph XXXXXXX

"Dear Mrs Stevens

I am the Wesleyan Chaplain who has pastoral charge of the Wesleyan and other nonconformists to the 3rd Battalion Coldstream Guards until they left us in February last.

Yesterday I had my first opportunity of revisiting them as they were 10 miles away from my division. It was a sad and trying experience and one of the greatest shocks of all was to hear that your son is numbered amongst the killed. My first enquiry was for him as I became greatly attached to him and had formed a very high opinion of his splendid character. He was ever to the foremost of rescuing the wounded and I understand was killed instantaneously in the performance of his duty in the recent great battle where his regiment fought so nobly and successfully. Alas! The price was very heavy. Your son was always present at my services on Sundays and week days when off duty. He frequently led us in prayer and his influence among the men was very marked. I shall never forget him and his kindly helpful friendship. I know that such men are the product of a fine home and clean beneficial surroundings and congratulate you in a son who was one of the bravest of all the brave lads who died – and not in vain – for England on that day.

May God comfort you,
Yours sincerely
W A Pannell."

HOLMER GREEN.
KILLED IN ACTION.

We regret to record that Pte. Martin Stevens, Coldstream Guards (son of Mr. and Mrs. George Stevens), was killed in action, in France, on April 13th. His parents, for whom much sympathy is felt, have received the following letter:—

31st May, 1918.
Dear Mrs. Stevens,—I am the Wesleyan Chaplain who has pastoral charge of the Wesleyans and other Nonconformists to the —— Battalion Coldstream Guards until they

THE LATE PTE. MARTIN STEVENS.

left us in February last. Yesterday I had my first opportunity of re-visiting them, as they were ten miles away from my division. It was a sad and trying experience, and one of the greatest shocks to hear that your son is numbered amongst the killed. My first enquiry was for him, as I became greatly attached to him, and had formed a very high opinion of his splendid charac-

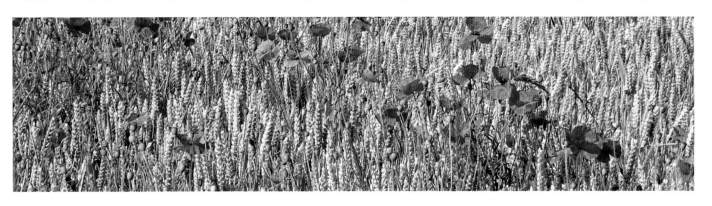

CHAPTER II

Richard Tilbury

Richard Tilbury's family first came to Holmer Green in the late 1820s when his Great Grandfather, also called Richard and from Hughenden, married a local girl, Elizabeth Puddifoot, and they settled to married life in Holmer Green. He was a butcher but became a farmer in later years – he was also a publican, having had the Bat & Ball built on land he had acquired.

Bat and Ball pub c1900, note tall hedge around the Common.

Molly Cribbes, neé Tilbury, long term pub landlady from the 1920s through to the 1960s.

Bat and Ball pub c1920s with the postman.

One of his sons, Henry, took up the local industry and became a woodturner, turning chair legs. An occupation that was followed by many men in the village – they were colloquially referred to as 'chair bodgers'. His wife, Mary Ann, was also following a traditional local occupation of the time – she was a lace maker.

Henry had 10 children. The third was James who also became a chair leg turner. In 1883 he married Mary Ann Ayres and they made their home in a cottage in Watchet Lane at the Wycombe Heath end of the village. Here they had 8 children and their third son was Richard, born in October 1888. Richard and his siblings attended the village school in Little Kingshill.

Richard was only 14 when his mother died in January 1903. Richard joined the army in 1908 and by 1911 when the census was taken, was overseas with his regiment. His widowed father, James, was still working at home in his cottage as a woodturner. James' unmarried sister, Fanny, was living there too and caring for the younger children.

The Tilbury family were well established in the village by now – the 1911 census shows that 8 of the 150 dwellings and buildings were occupied by Tilburys. Alfred and Annie were running the Bat and Ball, Fred and Alice

Ann Tilbury lacemaking on her lace pillow using typical style of wooden bobbins known as 'Bucks Thumpers'.

Langston's Cottage on the brow of 'Howe Hill', part of Watchet lane. This was originally a pair of cottages both occupied by chair bodging families, the Deans plus Henry and Mary Ann Tilbury-neé Ayres . This was Richard's birth place. The cottage was rented from George Stevens, Charles Dean's weekly rent being two shillings and three pence per week (equivalent to 11 new pence to-day) in 1900 with four weeks notice to be given on either side.

Cuckoo Cottage then and today, now known as April Cottage, in Penfold Lane.

were in Factory Street (now Orchard Way). 85-year-old Thomas was in Strawberry Cottage and being looked after by two of his young grand-daughters. Also retired were Alfred and Emily, living alongside 'Wood View' and retired farmers John and Mary Ann were living next door to Ivy Cottage whilst William and Sarah were living just along from James at Spurlands End. Next door to Richard's grandparents, Henry and Mary Ann, lived their daughter Ada with her husband, Horace Wright and their children

The ancient Peddles Cottage overlooking the Common, now the site of the Baptist Church.

Arthur 'Dan' Tilbury, Richard's Uncle, outside the front door of Peddles Cottage.

including a boy called Horace after his Father. He was Richard's first cousin and like Richard, Horace would also die in France, falling on the Somme in 1916, just a few days past his 19th birthday.

By the end of the Great War Richard's father, James, had moved from his cottage (Langston's) on Wycombe Heath to Cuckoo Cottage (affectionately named after his previous location), Penfold Lane on the other side of the village where it still stands and is now known as April

Peddles Cottage standing empty c1972.

Cottage. Sometime after this move Peddles Cottage overlooking the Common became their home, it has now gone and the new Baptist Church stands on the site. Today, nearly two centuries after they first arrived, there are many generations of Tilburys still living in the village.

1742 Estate map showing Peddles Cottage

The Tilbury family outside Peddles Cottage, some are identified below:
(1.) Henry Able Tilbury married in 1837 to (2.) Mary Ann – neé Ashald, (3.) Thought to be Fred Tilbury, born 1881.

Tilbury family c.1908 (Left –Right Standing) George Tilbury – Harry Tilbury – emigrated to Australia, Ada Tilbury – married to Will Page (Sitting) Elizabeth Tilbury   married to E Darvill, James Tilbury, Fanny Tilbury, James Tilbury.

Fanny Tilbury, she left home to work in service at Holmer Court for Sir Cecil and Lady Clementi.

Holmer Green Tennis Racket makers, Bill Deans, New Pond Road.

James Tilbury, father to Richard with his horse 'Betsy ' on Holmer Green Common.

'Offey' Tilbury, landlord of the Bat and Ball pub with members of the local Darvill family.

When he was 20 years old, Richard Tilbury decided to join the regular British army, signing up in High Wycombe on 1st September 1908 as a private in the newly renamed Oxfordshire and Buckinghamshire Light Infantry. Previously known as the Oxford Light Infantry, the regiment had evolved from the 52nd Light Infantry who had famously taken Napoleon's Old Guard in the flank at Waterloo.

Richard was initially with the regiment's 1st Battalion which was posted to India where it performed well in a number of actions. Later, Richard was transferred to the 2nd Battalion and was based back in England. At the out-break of war in 1914 they practised mobilisation exercises, little realising that they would shortly be involved in the real thing. On 13 August 1914, the 2nd Battalion embarked at Southampton on the SS Lake Michigan, landing at Boulogne the next day and moving to Mons, just in time to join the British Expeditionary Force as it made a necessary withdrawal and to form part of the rear-guard.

The regiment performed excellently through-out the campaign and every member was awarded the 1914 Star, also known as the Mons Star.

In May 1915, the unit took part in the second assault on Aubers Ridge, the first attempt having failed, and formed part of the southern arm of a pincer attack at Festubert. At 11.30pm on the 15th the attack went in with Richard's battalion on the right of the brigade, supporting the Royal Inniskilling Fusiliers. The initial attack was mainly successful and a stretch of the German's first line of trenches was captured and part of the second line too.

Richard Tilbury.

Richard Tilbury embarked at Southampton on the SS Lake Michigan on the 13th August 1914 for Boulogne.

The following morning the Germans opened rifle fire on the captured trenches, supported by heavy shelling which lasted all day until night fell at about 8.00pm. The regiment was relieved at about 1.00am in the early hours of 17th May and returned to its original breast-works.

A few hours later at 6.00am the regiment was ordered forward to occupy trenches just being vacated by the 2nd Highland Light Infantry as they moved to the attack. The enemy now heavily shelled these trenches throughout the 17th and many of the regiment's casualties occurred this day. The regiment was relieved just after midnight and pulled back to new billets to regroup and count the cost.

Over the three days the regiment had lost 5 officers and 47 men known to have been killed, 14 officers and 270 men wounded – and a further 3 officers and 61 men missing, making a total loss of 395 men. Due to the heavy shelling of the battlefield many of the bodies had been vaporised or destroyed by the fire and could not be recovered. We do not know exactly when Richard fell at Festubert but he was one of those missing men, registered as dead on 17th May 1915.

Richard Tilbury has no known grave but is remembered on the Le Touret Memorial in France. Richard's effects were valued at £19.3s.7d which

The Holmer Green Royal British Legion Standard lowered alongside the Holmer Green Heroes wreath, laid beneath Richard Tilbury's inscription at Le Touret.

The Le Touret Memorial, France..

was paid to his Father, James, on 3rd April 1916. James also later received a War Gratuity of £5.0s.0d, paid on 20th September 1919 – this had been calculated from the day war broke out through to his death, as a serving regular soldier his war service started on the day war was declared.

Two of Richard's brothers also fought in the war. His elder brother Henry – always known as Harry – had emigrated to Australia, sailing from Liverpool on 1st March 1911 on the Zealander bound for Fremantle in Western Australia. He enlisted into the Australian Imperial Force at Blackboy Hill, Western Australia, on 25 October 1916 and embarked for England on 23rd January 1917, arriving at Devenport on 27th March 1917. He was in the UK whilst the Australians reorganised and prepared for France – it is likely that it is during this time that Harry was able to return to Holmer Green and visit his family.

On 20th August 1917 they embarked for France and the fighting on the Western Front. Here, Harry was wounded by shrapnel in the face and neck on 4th October 1917 and was sent back to England for treatment, sailing on the Hospital Ship Warilda on 10th October and being admitted to the Bath War Hospital on 11th October. Harry was returned to Australia on 8th August 1918 for discharge due to blindness in the right eye.

Harry remained in Western Australia, marrying Pearl Patterson there and the couple had three children. Harry died in 1959 aged 73.

Harry Tilbury in his Australian Imperial Force uniform.

Harry visiting with his sister, Elizabeth – known as Nell – in Holmer Green during the war.

Pearl Patterson, wife of Harry.

C/o J.R.Patterson Cartmeticup Katannin W 22 – 4 – 23

Dear Charles,

    Was very pleased to hear from you again, haven't heard much news from the old village lately. I think that there is more news in your letter than I have had for the last twelve months, things must be looking up in H Green, guess the old pole lathe will soon be a thing of the past, haven't heard that you had got the engines in yet, but I suppose that is to come, guess a fellow won't know the place if he happens to get back there, expect by the time you get this you will soon be thinking about the fruit, does it look like being a fair season, would like to have a few weeks amongst the fruit myself, but no hope this time, but one never knows what the next might bring forth, the fruit season is just over here, fruit has been fairly cheap this season, haven't bought much myself as they have a garden with a good many fruit in it, it has been a very good fruit season.

    A bunch of grapes is very nice on a hot day, the winter is just starting here, it is raining outside now, have been waiting for the rain for some time now, as it is time to put the crop in now, and the ground is too hard to plough before it has had rain on it. We do the seeding in the winter here (it would be a contrast trying to put crop in the winter at home don't you think) but things are altogether different here.

Charles Dean.

    A lot of emigrants are coming out here now, I don't know if any are coming out from H Green, but I suppose everybody is doing well there now, I don't blame them for staying there, after all there's no place like home. Well I think this is about all this time now I close hoping this finds you all well as it leaves me, I remain your sincere friend H Tilbury

    P.S. Please remember me to all the neighbours, HT

George Tilbury, who was born on 17 April 1899, signed up for the Royal Navy on 23 April 1917, as soon after his 18th birthday as he could. What's more, he committed to a career in the Navy, signing on for a minimum of five years service and not just for the duration of hostilities. He was described as 5'5" tall with a 34" chest, light brown hair, grey eyes and a fresh complexion. His previous occupation was noted as Nurseryman.

George's first posting was to Pembroke – a naval training establishment – then, rated as an Ordinary Seaman, on 19 June 1917 he joined his first ship, HMS Penelope, an Arethusa class light cruiser based in Harwich as part of the 5th Light Cruiser Squadron. Penelope had already seen action having taken part in a raid on the German naval base at Hoyer in March 1916 as well as the hunt for the German ships that had shelled Lowestoft on 25th April 1916. Penelope had been torpedoed by a U-Boat but had made it safe home. Just before George joined her she had participated in the naval bombardment of the German base at Ostend.

A young George Tilbury.

In November 1917, Penelope was converted to carry 70 mines and carried out three highly dangerous minelaying trips.

George stayed with Penelope until 1st April 1919, having been rated as Able Seaman on 20 April 1918, just after Penelope transferred to the 7th Light Cruiser Squadron with the British Grand Fleet. Penelope, and presumably George with her, was present at the final surrender of the German High Seas Fleet at war's end.

George served on a number of ships and land establishments before his service ended in June 1922, passing his professional exams to be rated Leading Seaman in December 1921. His character was rated as Very Good by every one of his commanders and his abilities rated as satisfactory at every level of his achievements.

George married Florence Read in Wandsworth in late 1923 and they had two boys. George died in Kent on 10th April 1953, a week short of his 54th birthday.

Left and right: George Tilbury in his naval uniform.

On 19 June 1917 George joined his first ship, HMS Penelope.

CHAPTER 12

Horace Wright

Horace was born on 23rd January 1898 in Holmer Green – the eldest of four children born to Horace Wright and his wife, Ada Ann neé Tilbury. One of Ada's nephews was Richard Tilbury, first cousin to her son Horace and the first of our Holmer Green Heroes to fall.

The younger Horace's grandfather was William Wright who was born in Holmer Green in 1838 - William married Sarah Ann James – who herself was the Great Aunt of another of the Heroes, Wilfred James, who would be killed in August 1918. William and Sarah had seven children in their cottage in Factory Street, the fifth being Horace senior. William's father, also called William, was a sawyer from Hughenden who married Elizabeth, a Holmer Green girl and they settled here sometime in the 1830s. Their children and grandchildren became part of the village's chairmaking cottage industry – William and Horace senior were both chair leg turners with Horace working for Dancer and Hearn. Horace senior and wife Ada moved into a new semidetached house overlooking the common next door to the Tilbury family, he named this 'Green View' and it was the home of three generations of Wright's and it is still there today. By 1911 they had four children, Horace 13, Victor 10, Christiana 8 and Violet 6, there were also two borders, George 11 and Charlie Dedman 10, a household of eight. When the young Horace finished school he too became part of the trade –as an upholsterer, also like his father he was a very keen cricketer.

Ada Ann Wright neé Tilbury, wife of the above and caretaker of the Baptist Chapel just across the common from the family home, 'Green View'. This is a meeting with a commercial traveller in bibles and scripts, Mr Badder.

Horace Wright senior (top left) standing with his fellow chairmakers outside Dancer and Hearne's factory in Factory Street.

Horace was registered for the Army Reserve on 29th May 1916, four months after his 18th birthday. He was then formally called up on 18th October 1916 when he opted to join the Royal Navy and was assigned to the Royal Naval Volunteer Reserve 4th Battalion - a training unit. By this stage of the war, little effort was being made upon recruitment to send recruits to their choice of regiment or service as the need for replacements and reinforcements on the Western Front was critical. But, if a recruit or conscript asked to join the Royal Navy then the right to do so was protected and so the young Horace's request was granted.

However, since the Battle of Jutland on 31 May that year, the Navy's role was becoming one of blockade and convoy protection and the Senior Service had more men than it needed to deliver these roles. A new Infantry unit had been created earlier in the war – the Royal Naval Division – which had participated in the Siege of Antwerp and the Gallipoli landings in 1914 and 1915. This unit was now transferred to the British Army command as the 63rd (Royal Naval) Division. It had eight battalions, all named after famous Naval Commanders - Drake, Benbow, Hawke, Collingwood, Nelson, Howe, Hood and Anson – and the Division would serve on the Western Front for the remainder of the war.

Any dreams that Horace may have had of treading the decks of a fast destroyer or a dreadnaught were soon dispelled. Having completed basic training at Blandford in Dorset, Horace Wright was rated as Able Seaman and drafted to the Hawke Battalion on 2nd January 1917 and posted to join them with the British Expeditionary Force in France. Technically, Horace wasn't eligible for overseas posting as he wasn't quite 19 but by the time he joined his new unit on 26th January he had passed that milestone by

Young Horace in cricket gear

Victor, brother to Horace. Right: Victor (Vic) in old age and still living in the family house 'Green View'. Like most people in the village Vic was given a nick-name from a young age, it was 'Biscuit', but how this sobriquet was obtained is a mystery.

three days. His papers record him as being 5'4" tall with a chest measurement of 31" and weighing 100 lbs. He had a fresh complexion with dark brown hair and blue eyes.

Horace's cousin, Hubert, also fought in the war, initially joining the Oxfordshire & Buckinghamshire Light Infantry in 1916 and later transferring to the Royal Berkshire Regiment.

Before the war Hubert lived with his parents in Prospect Cottage on Beech Tree Road where he worked as a chair maker. Hubert married Marian Hatch in 1915 and when he returned after the war, they lived in The Homestead on the corner of Penfold Lane and Featherbed Lane.

The Hawke Battalion had just been relieved from a front line position in the trenches at La Vicogne and Horace Wright joined them in time to go with them on a long route march in extremely cold conditions to new billets at Forceville where they arrived at 5.30 in the morning of the 27th. However, their rest was short and at 3.15pm that same day they marched on to Lealvillers, arriving in the early hours of the next day which was spent resting and cleaning up.

Over the next few days the Division learnt of its part in the coming major attack, planned for early February, and the men of the Hawke Battalion were kept busy practising night manoeuvres and assaults on enemy held trenches.

Hubert Wright holding the tail and Bob Stevens on the corner of Featherbed Lane, taking a pig to be serviced.

Hubert Wright

Horace Wright

Operation Order No. 7 was issued to the Hawke Battalion on 31st January 1917, giving them their targets – the capture of the Puiseuix and River trenches. The order noted that the trenches and protective barbed wire had been very much damaged by shell fire, the morale of the opposing troops was poor and everything pointed to them being ripe for an attack. The Hood battalion would

Hawke Battalion cap badge

attack on the right and the Hawke Battalion on the left with the Nelson Battalion in support. The assault would be conducted in three waves with 80 yards between the first and second waves and 60 yards between the second and third.

At 4.30pm on the 2nd February they moved forward to the front line, relieving positions held by the Bedfordshire Regiment. At 7.00pm on the following day, the 3rd, they moved out to the start line in no man's land, lying down and covered by their greatcoats which they would discard for the attack. The British artillery commenced a preparatory barrage and at 11.00pm the assault commenced behind a creeping barrage which moved steadily towards the enemy trenches.

They initially met with little opposition, although a machine gun post threatened to hold up the advance but it was quickly silenced by two NCOs. Then a strong point was encountered and the right and centre companies split to go around it to complete the capture of River Trench – the left flank had already taken the Puiseuix Trench. The Hawke and Hood Battalions now consolidated their gains – setting up strong points on each flank and throwing out

machine gun outposts about 100 metres in front of their new position. At about 3.00am the enemy artillery started a very heavy shelling of the captured trenches but no counter attacks were launched until late afternoon. Thereafter, several German attacks were made and beaten off during the night of the 4th and throughout the 5th. The bypassed strong point had continued to hold out behind the new British line, surviving several attempts to capture it – it eventually fell to a major assault in the late afternoon of the 5th. The Battalion was relieved at this point and made its way back to billets to regroup.

That evening at 8.30pm, the Hawke Battalion reported having suffered casualties of 6 officers killed, wounded or missing and 59 other ranks killed, 87 wounded and 32 missing over the two days of fighting.

Horace had been reported missing after the first assault on the 3rd and his parents were now informed that he was missing in action. In August 1917 Horace's father requested that the Army investigate a report that a Seaman Wright was a patient in the Seaman's Hospital but this proved to be a different Wright and on 24th September 1917 Horace was posted as having been Killed in Action on 3rd February 1917.

Able Seaman Horace Wright died 11 days after his 19th birthday which makes him the youngest of our Holmer Green Heroes. He was killed only eight days after joining his unit in France and he was in the Royal Navy for just 108 days. He has no known grave and is remembered on the Thiepval Memorial on the Somme.

On Sunday 5th February 2017 Holmer Green residents commemorated the life and sacrifice of Able Seaman Horace Wright. Representatives of community organisations wait to lay wreaths at the village war memorial.

CHAPTER 13

Some returned home

■ Charlie and Rupert King

Brothers Charles (Charlie) and Rupert King both served in France and survived to live and work back home in the village and lived to a ripe old age. These lads came from a long line of farming stock; indeed, their parents and ancestors had farmed all five farms in Holmer Green plus others in Little and Great Missenden.

Edith (neé Morrell) and Rupert King

Charlie King

Kings Pond Cottage, Hyde End, The ancestral home of the King family.

Their ancestral line can be traced back to John and Elizabeth King living at 'Kings Pond Cottage', Hyde End in 1725, which still exists. The line continues through William b.1798 d.1875, Reuben b.1824 d.1908 and Charles b,1859, d.1927, farmer at Town Farm, Little Missenden from 1916.

News of this move to Town Farm was communicated to Rupert's brother Charlie serving in France via a letter full of interesting local news, it read thus.

Dear Charlie,

A few lines hoping to find you quite well. I am pleased to say I am pretty well, me keep mending steady. Mother is very sadly again, others all well.

Dear Chas, you be surprised to know that I have taken Town Farm, Little Missenden that Mr Elliot used to have. The whole lot, two hundred and 80 acres, the farm, castle, 3 cottages, 3 orchards, the fishing rights of the river Misbourne from Little Missenden Church to Suffocks [sic] bridge, also the watercress beds therein.

The sows have pigged, 1 has 8, 1-9 + 1-11, 27 lovely pigs I have. (Author's note: Charles' maths is a little out). The Barrow pig, he will be a monster by Christmas. I have sold the chestnut pony to Harry James for 7 pounds, I gave £5-15-0 for him. We make 4/0d of our butter and 4/0d a score of our eggs, bread 10d a 4lb loaf. Fat heavy old hens 4/- each, I sold 10 last week £12-o-o. I have nearly 300 fowl, 5 ducks and 1 drake.

Everything has gone deer [sic]. I have thatched my wheat in, it will get dearer yet if the war lasts. Little pigs are worth 25/- at 8 weeks down. Potatoes they say will be £20 per ton, Straw and hay are very scares and dear, no farmer is allowed to sell, only to the army without a permit, I had to get one from Aylesbury before I could get straw from J Lacey to thatch my reeks [ricks] in.

Leonard James came to me to see if I was going to give up where I am. He told me George Dean had been to Amersham to see if he could take it but it is no good anybody going there for years.

Charles King

The agreement for the farm I signed today, it states 300 acres, not 280, 60 acres rich meadows. I don't think upon reconsideration I shall give Tucker notice to leave the windmill, of course corn makes double what it did, make it not dear after all. The house would fetch 10-12 pounds a year and there always been a few pounds worth of fruit that with my field allotment would make a little place for one of my sons if they cared to have it.

So now dear Charlie, you must think that I have sent you a long letter and a lot of surprises which I think will interest you very much.

Dear Charlie, when you have read this, do your father the kindness, send this on to Corness in its entirety and tell him I will right to him shortly. Now I must conclude with fondest love to you and may the great God by whom you were created guard and guide you all and bring you safely back is the earnest prayer of your loving father and all at home, Charles King.

Note; Corness Otto King was brother to Charles and Rupert. The 'windmill' was situated in Watchet Lane, at this time the mill itself had been replaced in two other subsequent locations but the remaining house was still referred to as the 'Windmill' and today as Old Windmill Farm. There is an irony in Charles King's letter, on the one hand he is wishing that his sons come home safely, he must be aware by this time how terrible and dangerous this war is and on the other hand he appears to be pleased with the rising prices of his farm produce.

Town Farm, Little Missenden.

Charlie King, driver to a general in France.

Charlie joined the Royal Bucks Hussars yeomanry in 1907.

Being a farmer and owning his own horse Charlie joined the Royal Bucks Hussars yeomanry in 1907, for how long is not known. Charlie was serving in the Army Service Corp in France as a driver to a General, little else is known of his service history but like his brother Rupert he survived and returned, living much of his family life at 'Smarts Lodge' on the Hazlemere Park estate, the Lodge still survives today.

Rupert served in the Royal Artillery fighting on the Somme experiencing terrible death and destruction all around him, it was etched in his mind but, like many others, Corporal Rupert King would not discuss his gruesome experiences. Returning home, he settled back into Hollyberry Grove with his wife Edith whom he married in 1908 and lived a typically simple life of the times. He planted some of the new cherry orchards, he picked the cherries and was engaged in the general seasonal work of this still rural community.

Smarts Lodge at the top of Brimmers Hill, long time home of Charlie King, formerly part of the Leadbetter Hazelmere estate.

One unseasonal occupation kept Rupert busy, this was as the local grave digger. Rupert liked a pint and could often be found in the Earl Howe pub drinking with others and exchanging (and spreading) gossip. Most people in the village were related and one could often hear the greeting "ullo cuz, ow be an meart" (hello cousin, how are you mate"). It is recorded that on one grave digging job in the hard sticky Bucks clay, on a hot summers day with beer to sustain the hard graft, Rupert thought for a while that he had dug his own grave. He was found lying in his own excavation surrounded by empty beer bottles. worse for wear and had to helped out of the hole by a passing mate, Harry Mann.

Edith – who had been the church verger for over 40 years and responsible for ringing the single church bell on Sundays and at funerals – and Rupert, are both buried in Holmer Green church yard close to where they had lived most of their lives.

Rupert King in his cottage Hollyberry Grove.

Hollyberry Grove, note the rear bread oven.

Rupert's wife Edith with children (l – R) William (Bill), Jess, Edward (Ted) and Bess, both Bill and Ted would join the furniture trade.

Above; Five Generations of Kings (L- R). Rupert's son Ted, Rupert, Rupert's father Charles (in picture), Ted's son Stuart holding his young son Jason.

Holly tree at Hollyberry Grove.

◼ Johnny King

As noted by his daughter Daphne below, Johnny's passion was shooting, and not only on his own 'shoot' – he knew the area intimately and was not averse to shooting on the land of others to do a spot of poaching. This was not unusual in this rural location, indeed, it is said that everyone in Holmer Green owned a gun. Johnny King and many villagers like him saw this as a challenge against authority and of course a successful night netting rabbits or lamping pheasants provided extra food for the table, or a source of additional income from selling to a local butcher.

Tree felling in Penn Wood WWII.

Johnny King with a brace of pheasants.

Johnny King, right, with Timber Jill's in Penn Wood during WWII.

John, 'Johnny' King was a true village lad and country boy, the following sentiment was written by his daughter the late Daphne Rusin, neé King.

It had caused quite a stir when Johnny had been drafted to serve in the Gordon Highlanders during the First World War. On his occasional leaves he would return resplendent in the grand uniform of this Scottish regiment, responding good humouredly to the age old question "do you or don't you?" Perhaps this banter helped to avert deeper thoughts in those grim days, a period alienated from any other time in his life.

He returned from the war blending in benignly into his rural setting, retaining his genial sense of humour and canny country ways. A touch of the forelock and the usual greeting of "ow be an then?" reflecting his station in life, secure in the knowledge that he was home 'safe and sound'

The insignificance of his build and stature contrasted greatly with the character of his face and twinkling blue eyes and the ruddy weathered hue of his skin denoted his love of nature, and acceptance of all her elements. Strangely notable by their absence were the forefinger and middle finger of his right hand. Both had been severed in a threshing machine as he played and probed, many harvests ago on his grandfather's farm (Reuben King). This disability had not interfered with his activities. His firm and steady hands had mastered the intricate craft of hedge laying, the simple tasks of fruit picking and harvesting and had also saved many an animal from distress when in the throes of a difficult birth or sickness.

Dad's greatest pleasure was his 'shoot'. Clad in his old shooting breeches and gaiters, striped shirt, old shooting coat with large inside pockets – often used to conceal game shot out of season – his shabby workaday cloth cap aloft with his twelve bore shot gun under his arm, he would set forth to inspect his few acres of woodland (Beamond Wood). His duties were to trim and 'lay' hedges, fell surplus trees, control pests and curtail would-be trespassers. In return for these services he had been allowed the shooting rights, bagging the occasional pigeon or rabbit.

Although fully employed as a labourer, he gained great pride and satisfaction from his pastime and considered himself something of a gamekeeper. By contrast he would delight in pointing out the beauty of nature and derived great pleasure In taking a friend with him to watch the antics and frolicking of a vixen and her cubs in the soft light on evening. This velvet like gentleness was reflected in the small bunch of primroses, the pocket of mushrooms or a handful of nuts he would bring home for the children, also many a log of wood to add to a cheery fire.

Johnny had a Victorian attitude to family upbringing, a tone or a frown emphasising his approval or disapproval of a word or action, but the lively sense of humour which existed still strived and strained to escape through any chink in that strong armour. Many years hence I am reminded of a rare occasion when he put pen to paper. His sparse schooling had ill fitted him for this task but he had agreed to sign my autograph book, he wrote;

When the golden sun is sinking,
And your heart from cares set free
When of others you are thinking
Will you sometimes think of me?
How could I forget.

Johnny King, left, outside the Earl Howe pub in later years after his return from his wartime experience.

Poaching sketch by Norman King, son of Tom.

Penfold Lane, Johnny King had a wooden 'shooting hut' in Beamond Wood on the right.

Below is a press report of one of Johnny King's escapades. It is easy to trace his journey from the Little Kingshill pubs to his friend Frank Heather's house at Spurlands End, then along the Beech Tree Road and into Langley Farm. After killing the chickens he takes the footpath past the Rookery to the common.

Bucks Examiner report 1914, Great Missenden.

After the party was over
a drunken frolic and a costly one

At Great Missenden Petty Sessions on Monday, Jack King (John), labourer lodging at Holmer Green was summoned for stealing 16 fowls, the property of Ernest Thorn of Langley Farm, Holmer Green, the birds being valued at £6. Defendant pleaded "guilty".

The Case was tried by Mr Ernest Mathews (Chairman), Capt. Trevor Battye, Dr E.O. Turner and Mr Cecil Coombes.

Police-sergeant Benson (Amersham) stated that at 3p.m. on Sunday December 27th, in company with P.C. Baughan, he interviewed the defendant and said to him, "I am making inquiries respecting 16 fowls which have been stolen from Langley Farm, Holmer Green. Four of the birds are missing. I have reason to believe that you know something about it." In answer to [the] witnesses' inquiry defendant made a voluntary statement which he signed. The statement was as follows:- " My name is John King, and I am a farm bailiff. I left the Full Moon pub Little Kingshill at 9.45 p.m. on Saturday December 26 and went to the Prince of Wales until 10 o'clock. I then went to Frank Heather's and stayed there until 1a.m. next morning. I came out of there with Len Hawks who I lodge with at Holmer Green. I tried to ride my bicycle, but was unable to do so as I was under the influence of drink. So far as I could remember Len Hawks left me and took my cycle home. I can't remember any more as to how I got home, or when I

Ernest Thorn with farm workers.

got home. I am prepared to pay for the damage I have done.

Prior to interviewing the defendant witness, I visited the farm in company with P.C. Baughan and there found 12 of the missing 16 fowls which Mr Thorne had missed from his pen. Four of the 16 were not recovered. The birds had been killed by their heads having been pulled off. Ernest Thorne, the owner of the birds, stated that he was awakened at half past three on the Sunday morning, December 27th and looking out of his window he saw a man pass and go up the yard. It was moonlight and witness could see that the man was the defendant. Witness watched the man go through the gate into a field where there is a footpath leading to the cottage at which he lodged. The birds were valued at 7/6d each – £6 in all.

King stated that he visited public houses and had drink, and then had wine at a friends house, and when he left he was not sober. He afterwards ascertained that his friend had to leave him and go home with his bicycle, he had no recollection of what happened in the meantime. The Bench fined the defendant £5 and ordered him to pay £6 damages or 2 months imprisonment in default.

Langley Farm.

William Ives

We know very little regarding William Ives. We do know that his family were part of the local farming community around Little Missenden and thanks to his late younger sister, Doris, who lived in Parish Piece, Holmer Green, we have a few glimpses of his life. One charming glimpse is that of the extended family in their Sunday best at harvest time posing on a farm cart, but the most moving is a silk post card sent to his beloved father whilst serving in France. Will had signed up with the Queens Royal West Surrey Regiment.

It is likely that William returned home and at least for a time lived at the new family bungalow in School Lane (now Parish Piece). Doris was to live here until she died.

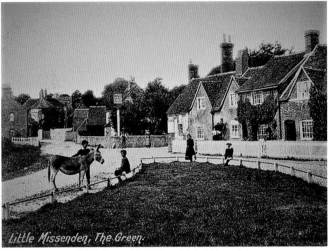

Will Ives with donkey, Little Missenden.

Will and Doris Ives on the tailgate.

Messages from the front

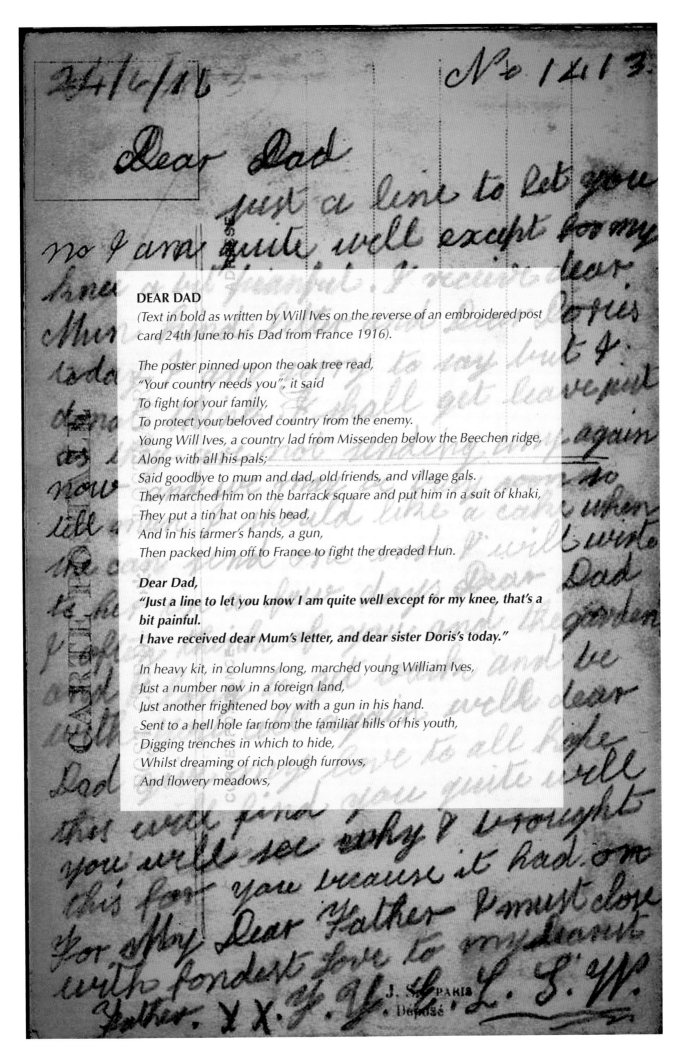

DEAR DAD

(Text in bold as written by Will Ives on the reverse of an embroidered post card 24th June to his Dad from France 1916).

The poster pinned upon the oak tree read,
"Your country needs you", it said
To fight for your family,
To protect your beloved country from the enemy.
Young Will Ives, a country lad from Missenden below the Beechen ridge,
Along with all his pals;
Said goodbye to mum and dad, old friends, and village gals.
They marched him on the barrack square and put him in a suit of khaki,
They put a tin hat on his head,
And in his farmer's hands, a gun,
Then packed him off to France to fight the dreaded Hun.

Dear Dad,
"Just a line to let you know I am quite well except for my knee, that's a bit painful.
I have received dear Mum's letter, and dear sister Doris's today."

In heavy kit, in columns long, marched young William Ives,
Just a number now in a foreign land,
Just another frightened boy with a gun in his hand.
Sent to a hell hole far from the familiar hills of his youth,
Digging trenches in which to hide,
Whilst dreaming of rich plough furrows,
And flowery meadows,

"I am sorry to say but I do not think I shall get leave quick, as they are not sending any more home again now, and we may be busy soon. So tell mum I should like a cake when she can send me one, and I shall write to her in a few days".

Will's trench was thick with mud and the stench of slaughter,
Once handsome estate bred horses lay rotting in a foot of water,
Accompanied by innocent young men,
Sacrificial heroes who give the lie to peace,
And on this post card young Will scribbled with his pen.

**"Dear dad, I often think of you and the garden,
and I long to be back and be with you all again".**

This bloody hell, this bloody Somme,
This bloody war to end all wars,
The bursting shells that never stop,
Will's post card, finished now,
Then over the top; another shell

**"Well dear dad, give my love to all, hope this will find you quite well.
You will see why I wrote this for you because it has on it.
"For my dear father".
I must close, with fondest love to my dearest father", Will**

Will Ives and Stuart King

Thomas Winter

The Winter family were farming at Wycombe Heath Farm and the general area for over 300 years and were very involved with the local community, none more so than Thomas Winter. Thomas deserted farming to become a schoolmaster, taking up teaching positions in several local villages including one as far as Bledlow Ridge – and he walked to each one. After a while a friend of his by the name of Timberlake hand-made a wooden bicycle, or more precisely, a hobby-horse (without pedals!). Thomas was regularly seen astride this contraption traveling between Holmer Green and High Wycombe, just one of his eccentricities. Upon his father Samuel's death he took to running Wycombe Heath Farm and so continued a long family tradition.

Being a superintendent of Holmer Green Baptist Sunday School and a keen and able musician, he formed the Holmer Green String Band in 1913 – made up mostly of village youngsters. So successful was the band that they were invited to play at the Crystal Palace, this was a journey of unimaginable excitement as life beyond the village for most of the youngsters was a rare experience.

Wycombe Heath Farm, Long time home of the Winter family, the last of whom were Thomas and Lizzie Winter (seen standing in inset c1900).

Holmer Green String Band c1913 with Thomas Winter standing tall in the back row in his YMCA uniform.

Thomas Winter relaxing at a cricket match.

At the commencement of WWI Thomas tried to enlist in the Royal Army Medical Corps but was rejected as his age of 59 years was evident. Undeterred this gallant member of the YMCA (Young Men's Christian Association) by his own volition served in Italy and France from 1915 to 1918 helping to relieve the suffering of troops. "It was always his practice whilst in Italy to try and walk the length of the troop trains to see if any local lads were among the Tommies, and by this method many were gladdened by a familiar face" (obituary).

After the war Mr Winter had a wooden hut built on the corner of Sheepcote Dell Road and the Common (known locally as 'Winter's Hut') for the use of the community. It served as a venue for the teaching of young girls the craft of tambour beading, a source of income for many a local 'gal', both young and old. Winter's Hut was also used as a young men's club and later as a general youth club and venue for other village events. The hut burnt down in the 1950s.

One of Thomas' claim to fame was that in his 76th year he walked from Holmer Green to London to visit his son Frank. A journey of 30 miles which took 10 hours, a feat that he repeated one year later exclaiming that, "I thought that I would just drop in".

In 1925 Thomas undertook a tour of the WWI battlefields and the following is an extract taken from a Bucks Free Press press-cutting dated 1925 of an article that he had written to the Editor.

"Crossing the country towards Albert is like the crossing of a desert, for there are no hedges, trees or anything to break the monotony of the view except several cemeteries here and there. In one of these, 'Beacon' by name, on examining the tombstones, I suddenly came to one that gave me many mingled thoughts and feelings for here was a dear boy from my village, Holmer Green, a boy whose name you have inserted in your cricket news many times, a member of the old Wycombe Heath Cricket Club.

Was his spirit hovering over me while meditating upon the many incidents we both experienced while visiting neighbouring villages for cricket? Who knows? I left with sad memories of by-gone days, but with a certain amount of thankfulness that this Gods Acre was so neatly kept and with such a profusion of flowers the whole being enclosed with a high wall for protection.

I am Sir
Yours Faithfully
THOMAS WINTER,
YMCA
Chateau de la Boulogne"

That "dear boy from my village" was Wilfred James. He is buried in the Beacon Cemetery in Sailly-Laurette on the Somme. In March 2016 four representatives from the village visited the grave where, with two Holmer Green Royal British Legion Standard Bearers present, held a short ceremony at Wilfred James' last resting place.

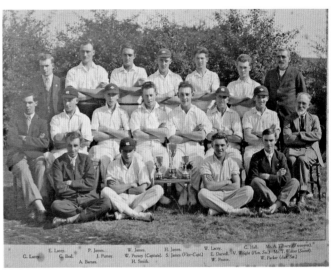

Holmer Green Cricket club 1928, Thomas Winter far right.

The Beacon Cemetery in Sailly-Laurette on the Somme with the Holmer Green Heroes wreath laid at Wilfred James' gravestone, March 2016.

CHAPTER 14

WWI Centenary Memorials

An important part of the Holmer Green Heroes project has been the memorial services and ceremonies that have been conducted to pay tribute to the fallen and remember them and their sacrifice.

In 2016, Stuart and Chris, together with the Holmer Green Royal British Legion standard bearers – Gordon Howland and Peter Rolt – visited every grave and memorial to our fourteen heroes. The trips took the team across most of the original Western Front in Belgium and France as well as two graves back home in England. Tribute ceremonies were conducted at every site and wreaths laid in remembrance.

On the centenary of each of their deaths, a memorial service and parade is being held in the village when eulogies to their lives are read, wreaths are laid and the villagers can gather to learn more about the heroes and their history. The first service was held in May 2015 and they will run through until the last one in October 2018, just before the centenary of the Armistice in November 2018.

Stuart King was chronicler and driver – snow wasn't in the plan for the Pilgrimage.

Private Wilfred James, Beacon Cemetery, Sailly-Laurette, The Somme.

Private Richard Tilbury, Le Touret Memorial, Pas-de-Calais.

Lance Corporal Ephraim Palmer, Houchin British Cemetery, Pas-de-Calais.

Major Merrick McConnel, Lijssenthoek Military Cemetery, Poperinge

Thiepval Memorial, The Somme – five of the village men are remembered here: Private George Cross, Private Frederick Haystaff, Private Charles Miles, Private John Miles, Able Seaman Horace Wright.

Private Ralph James, Westhof Farm Cemetery

Private Martin Stevens, Ploegsteert Memorial, Hainaut

Rifleman Harold Salter, Mont-Noir Military Cemetery, St Jans-Cappel.

Driver Ernest Salter, St Mary's Church, Haynes Park, Bedfordshire.

Private John Palmer, Christ Church, Holmer Green, Buckinghamshire.

The team were privileged to take part in the famous Last Post Ceremony at the Menin Gate, Ypres. Bugles played by local firemen have sounded the Last Post every evening since 1928 - this was the 30,240th occurrence.

The Holmer Green standards were paraded by Gordon Howland and Peter Rolt in front of a 600 strong crowd. Chris Peers laid a wreath to the Holmer Green Heroes.

The support from the local community has been tremendous – Councillor Graham Feltham, Holmer Green Senior School Head Teacher Michael Jones and Mrs Simmons of Christ Church – May 2015.

Michelle Peers, Sixth Form student at HGSS, gave the eulogy to Richard Tilbury – May 2015.

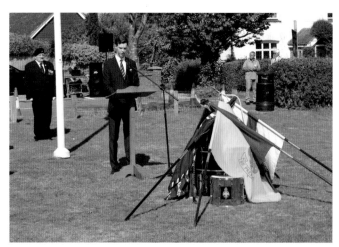

Matt Parminter, Sixth Form student at HGSS, tells of the family life of some of our Heroes – September 2016.

Ian Harvey lowers the Union Jack to half mast – July 2016.

Ian Harvey and Neil Spencer CBE, stacking drums and spreading Standards to make the Drumhead Altar.

Clergy from all three of Holmer Green's Churches have joined together to lead the ceremonies – here Peter Simmons, Christ Church, and Anthony Smith, Baptist Church, lead in May 2015.

Anthony Smith, Baptist Church, and John Richey, Methodist Church, lead in September 2016.

Anthony Smith takes the service in the Baptist Church in February 2017.

The young and the old remember together.

CHAPTER 15

After the War was over

Village life would never be the same, grieving families and friends were left only with memories of dear ones and often had to struggle without their practical support. Many of our lads returned home to pick up the pieces of a post war Britain, their lives had been changed forever with some coping better than others. Some of those returnees have been covered in previous chapters but there were many others of whom Arthur Ernest Barnes, Ernest Baines, Maurice Wingrove and Walter Fearless are just a few.

In common with communities countrywide a memorial was erected, ours situated in front of Christ Church facing the Common. At some stage the original stone cross was removed, maybe it became damaged? What is evident is that after WWII a simple stone obelisk replaced the cross and was erected on top of a new stone plinth with the names of the WWII heroes inscribed.

Holmer Green witnessed a boom in housing with much 'ribbon' development along such highways as The Beech Tree Road, Watchet Lane, Browns Road and Wycombe Road with former roadside fields being sub-divided into building plots. Fruit growing was starting to decline and chair bodging using the traditional pole lathe was having to compete with modern machinery. Many more men were being employed in the High Wycombe furniture trade, made easier with the recently introduced bus service.

By the mid-1920s the old school by the Common was replaced by a brand-new set of buildings in Parish Piece (this for a long time then became 'School Lane') to cater for all ages of children, taking also some children from surrounding villages. This is where our current story pauses, following the 'war to end all wars'? Let us once more remember and be thankful for our Holmer Green Heroes of WWI.

SK and CP

Maurice Wingrove: Lived at the Black Horse beer house, served in Egypt and became a Sunday school teacher upon his return.

Arthur Ernest Barnes: Left Holmer Green soon after 1919.

Walter Fearless: Durham Light Infantry, returned to the north as a Miner and died of silicosis. Pictured with wife Mirrian and daughter Edith .

Ernest Bains: Royal Warwickshire Regiment, born in Old Windmill Cottage and after the war became the Holmer Green School caretaker, lived at the 'Gables' for a time. Pictured with his wife Chrissie (neé Wright) and children L-R: Ella, Fred, Daisy and Ivy.

Dedication of the WWI war memorial.

Rededication of the War Memorial post WWII.